PENGUIN BOOKS

WHAT THE HELL IS HE THINKING?

Zoe Strimpel has been a journalist since graduating from Cambridge in 2004. She put her English degree to good use by writing features such as 'Can Men Fancy Talkative Women?', an experiment conducted while wearing short skirts and visiting Zoo Nightclub in Leicester Square. So conclusive were her tests – they can't – that Vanessa Feltz took her up on it on BBC Radio London. It was when she became *thelondonpaper*'s Girl About Town dating columnist in October 2006 that she began thinking about the peculiar behaviour of men in earnest. Her weekly columns prompted heated responses from London's commuters: women related; men reacted. She has since written on the odd relations between men and women for *Cosmopolitan*, the *Sunday Times Style* magazine and *The Times*, and has appeared on BBC One's *Sunday Life* as a spokesperson for 'freemales', women who genuinely enjoy the single life. She is currently the lifestyle editor for *City A.M.*

What the Hell is He Thinking?

All the Questions You've Ever Asked About Men Answered

Zoe Strimpel

PENGUIN BOOKS

PENGUIN BOOKS

Published by the Penguin Group
Penguin Books Ltd, 80 Strand, London WC2R 0RL, England
Penguin Group (USA) Inc., 375 Hudson Street, New York, New York 10014, USA
Penguin Group (Canada), 90 Eglinton Avenue East, Suite 700, Toronto, Ontario, Canada M4P 2Y3
(a division of Pearson Penguin Canada Inc.)
Penguin Ireland, 25 St Stephen's Green, Dublin 2, Ireland (a division of Penguin Books Ltd)
Penguin Group (Australia), 250 Camberwell Road, Camberwell, Victoria 3124, Australia
(a division of Pearson Australia Group Pty Ltd)
Penguin Books India Pvt Ltd, 11 Community Centre, Panchsheel Park, New Delhi – 110 017, India
Penguin Group (NZ), 67 Apollo Drive, Rosedale, North Shore 0632, New Zealand
(a division of Pearson New Zealand Ltd)
Penguin Books (South Africa) (Pty) Ltd, 24 Sturdee Avenue, Rosebank, Johannesburg 2196, South Africa

Penguin Books Ltd, Registered Offices: 80 Strand, London WC2R 0RL, England

www.penguin.com

First published 2010
1

Set in Bliss Light 10/14pt by Palimpsest Book Production Limited,
Grangemouth, Stirlingshire
Printed in England by Clays Ltd, St Ives plc

ISBN: 978-0-241-95278-8

www.greenpenguin.co.uk

Penguin Books is committed to a sustainable future
for our business, our readers and our planet.
The book in your hands is made from paper
certified by the Forest Stewardship Council.

To my parents, Harriet and Oliver Strimpel, who want me to end up happy more than anyone, be that married or single and loving it (well, they'd prefer married, to be fair)

Contents

Contents

Introduction

I was in the final throes of yet another quasi-dating thing, this time with a freelance website developer with all the time in the world for everything but me. Things had started off so promisingly. Our first date was the best I've ever had: a 48-hour cuddle-fest that had kicked off with a gorgeous meal and a romantic rickshaw drive through London to a fancy bar – all on him. But as time went on, and we kept seeing each other, things didn't develop as I'd hoped. When we were together (always having a great time) or, if I was lucky, in text messages, he would tell me that he missed me. But then days would pass without communication. There were so many mixed signals and contradictions, my head (and those of my friends who coached me through the whole thing) all but exploded.

In the end, things didn't work out. Why? I kind of got the sense he thought I wanted something too serious for him, but I couldn't be sure. As well as feeling sad it hadn't worked out, I was frustrated by the bizarre misunderstanding that seemed to have sprung up between us. What the hell had he been thinking this whole time?

Then a clever book called *He's Just Not That Into You* fell my way. For a moment, it seemed to make everything clear. All those intriguing contradictions and mixed signals? Those unsubstantiated moments of extreme affection? All signs that he was just not that into me. Great, case closed. And when a guy I had down for a rebound bailed on our first date because of 'a trip to Slovenia', I simply said to myself, OK, I get it. Not into me.

This new simple ethos was all very well until I realized it wasn't nearly enough of an explanation. I had a sudden vision of my friends and I sitting around with drinks, running out of boy-chat after six words, and promptly had a panic attack. No way would a six-word answer that entirely devalues and dismisses male thought or emotional subtlety be enough for me. I wanted to know what Rickshaw Boy (his name is Christian) – and all the other guys who say one thing and act out another – are thinking!

But why bother? Well, for a start, if someone I've spent some of my most intimate moments with suddenly appears to have jumped to another page, I'd quite like to know what page that is.

Then, I figure, once you know the page, you can get to know the book better.

Again, you ask, why bother? Isn't it enough to know that things aren't as they should or could be, and cease wasting time on them? Ideally, maybe yes. But life just ain't that simple. People – including men – ain't that simple. I mean, how often have we girls done one thing and, if pushed to think about it, meant another? Should we really just bin him because he doesn't ring when he says he will? Christ, it's going to be a long, lonely life if we're that black and white about everything. (Don't get me wrong, there's no excuse for shitty or, God forbid, nasty behaviour. Still, if you're reading this book, I'll wager you're smart enough not to get involved with anyone sinister.)

In the past, the rules may well have been clearer. There was a definite code of conduct. Neither men nor women were allowed to get away with inhabiting the grey area of romantic intentions many of us do today. Judging from the way my grandmother talked on the Sunday afternoons I'd pay my weekly visit, there was a time when a girl was perfectly entitled to assume a guy had marriage on his mind from the moment he showed interest. Now, as she was bewildered to learn, that guy I've been seeing might not even be a boyfriend, and almost certainly won't become a husband. Plus, I had to explain, there are so many fancy ways to interpret his grey intentions. We've got Facebook antics, texts, email, MSN and jobs so cut-throat many of us like to think we don't have time for commitment. Our lifestyles are now so replete with choice and independence that our interactions with the opposite sex have simply become another form of both. Commitment flies in the face of the contemporary dream, I would explain. So if relationships are complex at the best of times, modernity has thrown an added veil over our dealings with one another. What the hell we are truly thinking and feeling can be anybody's guess. 'Good heavens,' Grandma would respond. 'I'm glad I'm not out there looking for a man now.'

But, modernity or not, we still want a good bit of loving. And I genuinely believe that men – hateful creatures as they may sometimes be – are worth trying to work out. Wouldn't we like to get a little closer to knowing what the hell he's thinking? I, for one, value the male presence in my life enough to want to know.

By 'working out', I don't mean we're going to find all the answers. The world of dating and relationships doesn't really lend itself to an exact science. Nor am I a guru. I am a normal, frazzled, fun-loving but responsible twenty-something trying to make sense of the romantic wilderness from whose branches I'm currently swinging.

But my girlfriends and I weren't getting any closer to the truth by talking among ourselves over still more cocktails. So one day, it occurred to me that I could just ask a bunch of guys why they do the things they do. After all, for the year and a half that I wrote my weekly dating column for London morning newspaper *thelondonpaper*, the most impassioned, articulate and frequent respondents were men. Guys wanted to put their two cents in on the dating thing: they thought about it too, and obviously felt that their voices weren't being heard. So I figured there was a lot of manpower to harness out there. And, as predicted, they were more than happy to divulge.

This book isn't about streamlining the search for The One, nor is it a self-help book. It's a conversation with men, who, judging from the honesty and keenness with which most approached my questions, are as eager as we are to bridge the knowledge gap.

In the quest to find out what the hell he's thinking, I've talked to dozens, if not hundreds, of men. I asked them for their views in two formats, which I believe are the best ways of gleaning the information and insight most women are after. One is explanation: getting them to respond to accounts of flummoxing (but – to most women – recognizable) male behaviour, such as that of Christian above. Thanks to the candour of the guys I asked, I was able to see what was going on with Christian, with some clarity, and why. How could I have known he was a 'classic Casanova' – that is, addicted to making girls love him for the resulting feeling of validation – if it wasn't for Adam Lyons, a top pick-up artist and dating coach? Or that Christian, no matter how genteel, polite and charming he was when we met up, was not above the 'why buy the cow when you can get the milk for free' line of thinking? That is, while I was busy trying to impress him with my easy-going coolness, and wondering when the penny would drop about how great I am, he merely saw me as someone who didn't demand anything more challenging than a bottle of nice booze when we met, in exchange for sex, cuddles and all manner of ego flattery.

The other format is simple 'quick-fire questions' about all that stuff you've always wondered, from the lowliest physical question such as 'Do tampons make you queasy?' to 'How important is it to you that your friends think your girlfriend is attractive?' and 'Would you rather date a stupid but beautiful woman than a humorous, intelligent but less gorgeous one?'

These questions and their answers come at the end of each part of the book, so they correspond in some way, sometimes loosely, with the preceding chapters. 'Commitment Phobia' for example, begs the bite-sized but still revealing question 'What's the biggest thing a girl does that scares you off?' as well as 'Do you wish you could have a polygamous relationship?'

Inevitably, there is some overlap – after all, we're talking about love, lust and all the things in between, so nothing is too clear-cut. For example, although I decided to make 'Sharing Space' its own section, some of the questions following it relate to commitment phobia, such as: 'What's so scary about moving in with someone?'

Now, about the guys on the *What the Hell is He Thinking?* panel, the guys whose voices are our conduit into the male mind. They are all articulate, smart, thoughtful and basically good guys. I didn't interview thuggish men or overt misogynists, because this book assumes that we're talking about guys who deserve to be analysed, thought about and figured out, even if relationships with them don't work out or they behave like arse-wipes. I am not interested in telling you something about all the men in society; just about the ones I reckon you're likely to date, fall foul of, be mystified by and – one day – maybe stick with.

Particular stars on the panel are Tom L, recently out of a four-year relationship with an excellent woman he fell in love with on first sight; Anthony A, an adorable, woman-loving Lothario who I once snogged but am very glad did nothing more with; Victor L, my ex-flatmate's boyfriend, who can talk for hours with scary brilliance about relationships and did so in our living room on many occasions; and last but not least, Adam Lyons, who, despite being a busy professional dating coach and pick-up advisor, managed to lend his eye to lots of the cases presented here and always cut through the complexities with his scarily shrewd, and often cynical, insider's perspective on the male mind.

There are, of course, a variety of responses here; not every man said the same thing (that would just be weird). But the more I collated them, the more I got a flavour of the way men think. It's not something that can be explained in a sentence – though many people try to do that with such statements as 'men are cowards' or 'guys are straight-forward; there's no point reading too much into their actions'. Although those opinions might contain some truth, there are so many exceptions that they aren't particularly helpful. Gaining a flavour of the way men think, on the other hand, *is* helpful, in the same way that learning a language takes more than a few short grammatical lessons. You have to pick a language up, gain a feel for it.

I hope that once you've read this book (and it is fine to cherry-pick the chapters; you don't have to read them in sequence), you'll have a feel for the rhythm of the male mind, and when inexplicable behaviour comes your way you'll be able to better understand what's going on. The name of the game is not to be thrown when a guy does something weird; rather, to recognize what it might mean, and where it's coming from. This should empower you to respond sensibly: to either persevere effectively or throw in the towel. Either way, knowledge is power. Here's to both. Oh, and having a whale of a time.

PART ONE
Commitment Phobia

If I had to choose the single most influential idea in modern dating I would say it's a no-brainer: commitment phobia (let's call it CP for short). Oh yes, that spectre of budding relationships, the two words that sum up everything terrifying that could happen to a horny young or youngish stud or minx: cohabitation, marriage, kids, entrapment, not sleeping with anyone else ever. Both sexes feel it, and both try to pre-empt it by elaborate displays of independence and froideur. The desire not to seem too keen or – God forbid – needy is overwhelming in dating today.

CP is basically a weird mental construct. It's a presumption that things could and therefore will turn out a certain way. It takes a worst possible scenario (the death of freedom) and makes it the most likely. It assumes the other person is deadly serious and about to call the vicar after three dates, causing you/him to run a mile. It's also profoundly narcissistic: only someone who thinks they're all that is convinced everyone they date could well be falling into a lifelong obsession with them and hatching a plan to take over their life.

Sometimes this feeling of 'help, get me out of here' is fair enough. Nobody likes to feel smothered when they aren't sure of their feelings. If the other person makes an effort to reign in his or her keenness it can increase sexual tension and prevent the deadly smothered feeling, possibly leading to something good.

But the big mystery to me, and I believe to a lot of women, is how random and unrealistic a lot of guys are with their CP – how they can assume they're about to be roped into something awful when all you did was call them. And what's up with guys keeping us at arm's length for months, refusing to call us their girlfriend, or treat us like one, because God knows having a girlfriend is the most toxic state out there? Frankly, it gets in the way, men and their stubborn, capricious stabs of CP. And it's bloody annoying when they treat your simple desire to say hello the morning after a night of snogging as a sign that you plan to stalk them – when in fact you may be even less up for it than them.

This section tackles what lies behind male CP and will hopefully empower you either to treat it with the scorn it often deserves or to recognize deeper issues and work through them. Sometimes you might think the guy has self-aggrandizing CP, when in fact it's just his garbled way of showing you he isn't keen so that you won't blame him (and he can't blame himself) later for having led you on. It can be a sign of misguided honesty.

The most obvious kind of CP – the type we've all either faced or dished out – rears its head at the very beginning, in the first few months of dating. But there are other types, more worrying versions, such as in Steve, the guy who reliably ruins relationships at the one-year mark. What's he playing at? And what about the guy who won't even commit to his wife – or indeed to his mistress? Read on to find out, then see a bunch of guys' answers to related questions, ones you've always probably wondered about (I have, anyway), such as 'What do you think about public displays of affection?'

Ahh, sweet, sweet enlightenment.

1

Why does he string you along for three months, then cut it off?

THE CHRISTIAN FILES

Years of hooking up with the wrong guys has made me pretty cautious of 'commitment'. 'Commitment' is not something a lot of guys like the idea of either. It's a 'scary' thing, a kind of humourless, cramping state leading to babies, sexual boredom and – eww, gross – responsibility. Who wants that? Well, not me (yet). But like most sane girls, I don't automatically associate the C word with all of the above. I don't see why, if something is going well, turning it into a proper relationship is necessarily such a fearsome idea. This isn't the Middle Ages. Giving something a go isn't the death of freedom for ever. After all, we're not demanding an electronic tagging system be fixed to his ankle so that we can monitor his every move. We don't want to spend every waking hour together. We just want to have fun and feel happy. Plus babies would really, really cramp our style just now. So from whence the fear-factor boys?

Here's a classic case: a recent thing I had with a 27-year-old website developer (the guy from the Introduction, yes). It never really got off the ground, although I'm convinced it would have been nice if it had.

THE CASE

OK. So here's why it could have been good. We met at a party. Or, I should say, I saw him, thought, 'You're cute' and leapt on him. Minutes later we were out in the garden, away from everyone else, kissing. And kissing. Really top kissing, too. An hour passed in what felt like a minute – I kiss a lot of guys and this was something else. He actually asked me if I was single. 'Wow!' I thought. 'He's serious!' I invited him to come back with me and he was a pure gentleman, quietly paying for the cab, refraining from sex (I was a little disappointed by this) and the next morning asking when he could call me.

The next day I had an email from him inviting me to dinner and drinks that Friday night. I was stunned – it's not every day a guy goes for the top-drawer slot: Friday *and* dinner. It turned out to be not just any dinner either: a posh restaurant in Mayfair, if you please, then a swanky bar in Soho. Chivalry aside, he put me at my ease, we chatted with gay abandon and he had all the moves. We ended up spending the entire weekend together, unable to move from his bed.

Now, call me crazy, but a 48-hour first date bodes well. So imagine my surprise when we parted ways at the Tube station on Sunday evening with a chilly 'Don't be a stranger' from him. And then, when I hadn't heard anything from him by Wednesday, and thinking I had nothing to lose, I emailed, thanking him for a nice weekend and making general chit-chat. His reply was all smiles, and he offered to come round that Friday with chocolate cake. Again, we had a gorgeous time, as chocolate cake led to drinks. The following Saturday we went to the races.

Things continued in this stately and systematic vein: no excess communication, carefully planning things in advance. At our peak, we saw each other twice a week, but I couldn't shake the feeling that things were always in danger of going slack. I also couldn't help but wonder what would have happened if I'd never emailed that first week. All this aside, I was dizzy with excitement when he texted from Paris to say that he 'might be missing' me (a month in).

I kept waiting for the week he'd start really gearing things up – you know, coming round for DVDs on the spur of the moment, etc. It didn't quite arrive, even though our dates were always lovely boozy affairs. Time slid by. I really fancied him. After three months I began to feel helplessly upset and disappointed that he wasn't in touch more than every four days. At one point (end of month three) I explained that I was upset – the only time I ever did – that he hadn't seen fit to let me know he wasn't going to be back for the weekend and hadn't been in touch for five days. He mumbled apologies, then did the same thing the next week, admitting he was proving a point. He explained, 'There might be times when I'm away and I can't be in touch every day or whatever.' This was a couple of weeks after he had said, with a caress, in bed, 'I can't have a GIRLFRIEND. I told myself I wouldn't, so I could focus on freedom and work' (or something to that effect).

So there's me, offering my best, not demanding much, fun to be around, and he's pushing me away in case I become a GIRLFRIEND – evidently a poor trade for total unaccountability – or freak out if he doesn't call every two seconds when he's 'away' (what kind of precautionary point is that?). To make matters more confusing, the week before all this point-making he had bought me a toothbrush so that I could brush my teeth at his. This would normally be regarded as a commitment-esque gesture, no?

But then he stopped planning things, and would call to ask what I was up to that same night. Which is fine, if it goes hand in hand with plans. I started to feel that if I didn't drop everything I might never see him again so I tried to be available when he called.

The moment I left his flat one Wednesday afternoon after an

impromptu sleepover (the possibilities are endless for two freelancers), with that now-familiar sinking feeling that I didn't have a clue when I'd next see him, the penny dropped. It was time to end things. I'd clearly gone from claiming weekend slots to spontaneous mid-weekers when I really should have been working. I decided to ignore his calls. It was easy, since they didn't come. Then, three weeks later, a casual 'What's up' message arrived on my voicemail – no reference to the silence just bridged – and finally I had my chance to not call back.

Christian and I got on. We definitely had a lovely time together. We had terrific physical chemistry. No surprise then that after three months I wanted more than strings-free hanging out. I couldn't help it. Why could he? And why did he find it so easy to adhere to some self-imposed rule about girlfriends instead of yielding to the situation? I was offering the next step from casual dating, because it didn't feel purely casual to me any more. It was the obvious next step – not marriage. Was I mad? Was he secretly repulsed by me?

WHAT THE GUYS THINK

According to a clutch of my far-from-angelic male friends, Christian did not act like a nice guy. All the same, they knew where he was coming from.

As I've always suspected, and as this book assumes, men are not animals that act purely on impulse and the penile imperative. They are smart, and, contrary to received wisdom, there can be complex motives to their odd behaviour.

TOM L, 28, RECENTLY SINGLE

Tom is one of my loveliest male chums, but when it comes to women he hasn't always been Mr Nice Guy. Here's what he had to say about Christian's near pathological phobia of commitment – and overall nutcase behaviour.

Smart animals

'Unlike dogs, men can and do read what's written about them, so they also know how to manipulate perceptions. The toothbrush, for instance, is a classic move: for a man it just means convenience. But men also know that women have imbued the toothbrush with a wildly disproportionate significance. That makes it an easy way to accumulate romantic capital. Buying a woman a toothbrush means he doesn't have to make any other commitment gestures for quite some time.

'But – just like animals – men are motivated by self-interested simplicities. There's that saying about not wanting to buy the cow when you get the milk for free, and I suspect that plays a large part in Christian's behaviour.'

Basically, I proffered the booty on a plate, so he didn't want the rest.

Sex sans commitment

'This sounds like a relationship that was defined by sex right from the beginning. Clearly there was a spark between your personalities, but the whole thing may have led to the down and dirty side too quickly. True, he himself prolonged the final consummation, but it sounds like the option was very much laid on the table from the beginning. He must have thought it was a done deal.

'There's something to be said for that advice from the older generations, that there can be an upside to holding out. I mean, look at Anne Boleyn in The Tudors: her sister was effectively fucked and chucked, but Anne coyly holds out until she's brought down not only Henry's marriage, but the entire edifice of the Catholic Church in Britain.'

But withholding sex isn't quite the thing either

These aren't Tudor times, and sex has been made acceptable common currency in male–female relationships – sometimes it can actually be simpler to say yes than no.

'Of course, there is a danger in holding out,' admits Tom. 'Under ideal circumstances it means the guy has to get to know you better, has to reflect on how much fun you are, etc., and comes to think of you as a friend as well as a sexual partner. Under grim circumstances he gets bored and heads elsewhere.

'Holding out is a difficult balance to get right: Basically, if you think you're getting on like a house on fire and there's plenty of sexual tension, then there probably is, and a little holding out might work.'

So

'He's a dickhead,' says Tom. 'While it suited him he was more than happy to keep the relationship going, and pulling all the tricks he'd learnt from reading girlfriends' copies of *Cosmopolitan*: letting the toothbrush in, little texts from Paris, etc. But when it didn't suit him, he would let it slip.'

Couldn't have said it better myself.

ADAM L, 31, IN A COMMITTED RELATIONSHIP

Tom's no stranger to the dirty tricks men sometimes play – but basically he's a nice guy. I thought it would be worth talking to a pro, someone scarily well versed in the tricks men play, and one who's tried most of them out himself. Enter Adam Lyons, the world's third-ranked pick-up artist and professional dating coach.

Casanova

Like Tom, Adam says I've been had. He has divided ladies' men into three types of pick-up artist, and Christian falls perfectly into the Casanova category. Casanovas teach themselves how to make women fall for them because they weren't always the smoothies they are now. They get off on the validation of getting it right over and over, but don't care about a long-term result – and they're cold perfectionists. So, according to Adam:

'The toothbrush, romantic texts, the dazzling dinners and champagne are classic touches he has developed through rigorously studying what makes women get attached. He probably started styling himself as a Casanova once he got out of his awkward spotty phase but still hasn't quite forgotten the early days of rejection. Guys like this get totally obsessed with their game and forget that at the end of the day there's a potential partner at stake.'

So

He's a grade A, archetypal pick-up artist of the Casanova variety – unfortunately the most dangerous of all. Like me, you often don't realize you're being had until it's too late and you're hooked.

BOTTOM LINE

Guys that hold you at arm's length to a cruel and mystifying extent are not good news, because they are motivated by some internal, hidden game with themselves – their main concern is to hone their moves. You – as a lovely, energetic, smart and fun person with a lot to offer – barely come into it. That said, there was a sex-on-a-plate element to which he was not impartial. Tom says, 'Christian was just in it for the booty.' What's sad about that – and Tom puts it beautifully – is that 'he was evidently not yearning for the human interaction that's at the heart of any truly permanent meeting of hearts and minds.' (Isn't Tom a darling?) Early sex doesn't have to cancel out the potential for a relationship, but it can – as it did here – get in the way of a guy appreciating the woman herself. 'I think that's a problem women don't have,' says Tom, 'but it does sound to me like you fell victim to it with Christian. And that means you're better off without him.'

What to do if you fancy a Christian: Be very, very clear with yourself that this is about keeping up an act: champagne and nice dinners, sex and cuddles that mean nothing (to him). If you feel yourself being drawn into his web – and only a Samantha Jones-type could resist – pull yourself out before the aching misery and frustration that Christian made me feel seeps into your life. Oh, and order the most expensive thing on the menu every time. If he's going to extract a high emotional fee for your services, you can cost him a lot too. Of Moët.

2

Why does he go weird the day after, teenager style?

THE JEREMY FILES

Commitment phobia rears its head in all kinds of ways in all kinds of men, regardless of whether commitment is actually on the cards. OK, often a guy senses correctly that you would like things to be a little more serious. When he goes weird, you have no choice but to go on your merry way, or make a fool of yourself.

It can be sad, that moment of pre-emptive cooling off from a man to whom you're getting really rather attached. What's not sad – just funny and baffling – is when you get the cold water poured on you in a fit of what looks like and smells of commitment phobia, before a relationship of any sort has even got off the ground. See, the old jig of not talking to the girl you snogged the day before died before most of us got to college.

So imagine my surprise to discover it's still alive and well among certain 31-year-old gentlemen who really should know better. At this stage in the game, what on earth could be going through a man's head to make him think that a snog and a fumble one drunken night means that by the next morning the snogee will assume she's got rights to the next ten years of his life?

THE CASE

I was at a friend's wedding in France earlier this year. As the party wore on and drunkenness increased, various potential hook-ups for the night swirled into view. I was just about to close the deal with Tim, a sexy friend of the groom who I'd met a few times before, when suddenly Jeremy cut in, dragged me away for a dance, then dragged me outside to the bushes.

Now, I could have resisted, obviously. But I'd long quite fancied Jeremy, beginning with a party at my friend the bride's place a couple of years ago. He's handsome and buttoned up in that deeply civilized, sexy way that hints at tragic repression and pent-up sexual energy. We hit it off back then, but alas, he didn't seem interested and I forgot about him.

So I was surprised when he leapt on me at the wedding, and I gave in for old times' sake. I didn't feel much while we snogged in the bushes, and eventually pulled myself away, highly amused.

I have to be honest, though: I'd have given it more of a chance, because he's a quality guy. One dud drunken snog does not a door close.

Nor, however, does it fling one open. So, next day at lunch, the furthest thing from my hungover mind was Jeremy and what he was thinking. A wedding snog is so standard you can barely read into it. All the same, it's a shared experience and you expect a little chuckle with the other guilty party. Not blanking. When I walked into the restaurant, I saw Jeremy and smiled, thinking we could have a bashful chuckle. If the flirtation continued apace, well, I'd be open to that too. Instead he went bright red and looked violently put out. He was embarrassed, yes, but not in a friendly, has-a-crush way. Chat was painful, so after I said hi I moved away as fast as I could.

I tried being friendly later in the day before we all left, thinking maybe his hangover had crippled all social faculties and sent him back to school-age. No, he was just as cold and unfriendly, only this time without the blush. Later that day he did text something awkward but friendly, with reference to hangovers and tired dancing legs.

It's not that I was expecting anything or even conscious of wanting anything. I was just utterly thrown by being blanked the next day, even though he'd been the one to go for it. He's a talkative, sophisticated guy who has had girlfriends before. What made him act like a nervous teen? I had intentionally been friendly to show that we were cool.

WHAT THE GUYS THINK

JAKE K, 34, IN A LONG-TERM RELATIONSHIP

Jake is the strong, quiet type but he can deliver pretty scathing truths about the way men think. He doesn't say anything we haven't heard before, but he says it convincingly, and with great knowledge. His big thing is about guys and their prey (you). Once they've got what they want, there is no end to their boredom/rudeness/callousness.

OK, I've got it now

'It's a hunting thing,' Jake starts, slightly worryingly. Hunting? Really? A nice guy like Jeremy?

Apparently. 'Once you've got your prey you're like, "OK, I've got it now." Then you're over it. Men are really competitive – it doesn't matter what kind of man. He saw you dancing with other guys and thought, "I can have that too." But rather than show he liked you in public, he isolated you and took you out to the bushes – he wasn't up for anything beyond a quick physical incident.' Ouch. He didn't want to be seen with me because if his mates saw us it would immediately become more.

Embarrassment

'Why does he go cold? Embarrassment, plain and simple. He's a nice guy and wants to hide from his mistakes – he's fully aware he went for you for the wrong, selfish reasons. When he'd met you before the wedding, he'd decided not to go for you, then he went back on himself.' Great. Once again, the guy is in some big melodrama about having done something bad/wrong/unintended, while I'm just up for saying hello the next morning. (And maybe the morning after.)

'The main reason men avoid women is guilt – they remind them of their mistakes. That was you the next morning. But the fact that he texted shows he's a nice guy.'

So

Jeremy was motivated to snog me by nothing more than sudden competitiveness – or some irrelevant urge – when he saw I was up for grabs elsewhere. So the next day he regarded it as a mistake, since there were no feelings there. And, as he was a well-heeled thirty-something, he probably didn't feel comfortable with behaving like that. Men find it very difficult to face their mistakes in female form and because he's quite nice, he probably felt guilty when he saw me. Another reason to avoid me.

MARK M, 25, IN A LONG-TERM RELATIONSHIP

Mark is perfect boyfriend material: sweet, adoring, considerate and the kind of guy you can't imagine running screaming from a girl for very little apparent reason.

Fear

'This behaviour is always extremely confusing to women. The thing is, even men who aren't typically bastards sometimes behave like them without realizing it.' That sounds about right, but the whole clueless 'I didn't know I was being a bastard' thing is annoying and a function of not being self-aware. We know perfectly well when we're being mean, don't we, ladies?

'It's mainly to do with fear.' Fear! Again! Men – it appears – are very easily scared. Much more easily than us. Much. 'And in this case fear of confrontation. Men want to avoid discussion about what happened the night before, or any tricky situation, at all costs. That chat in the morning may have been painful for you, but it will have been even more painful for Jeremy. Men are terrified of being asked to give straight answers to any direct questions about their romantic intentions or feelings, or indeed lack of them, towards women. I think that would explain the morning-after behaviour, while a hangover is sure to exacerbate any anxiety.' Ah yes, the fear of the straight answer. Well, nobody likes to put someone down, but men – especially the nice ones – seem to dread it morbidly. That would explain the issue of men driving a relationship off the bridge rather than stopping it and getting out before it reaches the edge. But why?

Vague instincts

'The reason a guy doesn't want to be asked any direct questions is that he doesn't have any answers. Men are extremely inarticulate when it comes to emotions. So they'll just try and avoid the whole situation by blanking it out.' This is primary-school tactics.

'Men often act first in the name of sex, and think later. Before Jeremy kissed you, he was not thinking for hours about whether he just wanted a snog or a relationship or trying to assess how much he likes you, he was being driven by a basic, primal instinct: he wanted to have sex. And even this thought may be too fully formed. Men generally act on very vague instincts, rarely stopping to reflect on what might be behind them.' So what seems to happen is that guys don't think at all at first, then make up for it with overthinking, fear and melodrama afterwards. We keep a more even balance between thought and action throughout. And now for the cold truth:

'Jeremy hadn't spent the night soul-searching about what he wanted with you, but something told him that he didn't want anything between the two of you to get even remotely complicated.' That fear of complication again, as though it's a mind-and-body-breaking mathematical task.

Not quite commitment phobia

A final thought: 'This smacks of commitment phobia, I know. But it's more that an element of doubt comes into your head, however small, and then you know you just want to remove yourself from this situation before anything can develop.

'It's true that in general men do assume that women are all after relationships, so getting involved with someone, even casually, is always a bit scary.'

So

A vague sense of physical impulse motivated him to bring me out to the bushes. He knew right away he didn't want anything else and – more to the point – he didn't want to hint that he did to me. To be sure I didn't get the wrong idea, he acted as coldly as possible, terrified of landing himself with a complex situation.

BOTTOM LINE

Jeremy reacted as he did out of a mixture of cringing discomfort at being faced with a guilty 'mistake' and a desperate need to show me that nothing further would happen, to avoid complication. That he saw our hook-up as a mistake is testament to his so-called gentlemanly idea of himself; also to the fact that men get a little dramatic about this kind of thing. To run screaming from potentially complex or challenging situations with women is a trait that runs the gamut of guys. His fear of such a situation with me was – like so much else with blokes – a product of his assumption-breeding, fearful mind, not my actions.

What to do if you fancy a Jeremy: Steer clear of him. Guys behaving all stand-offish like Jeremy are enacting a version of damage control. Snogging/shagging you was the damage. There are no feelings, only a desperate desire to make that fact clear. Therefore the 'get away from me' vibe will hysterically increase if you apply any pressure, and decrease the more you leave him alone. In fact, your blatant show of disinterest might start to play on his mind: you'll once again become the prey (as Jake bangs on about), and maybe he'll go after you again, possibly more genuinely. Don't hold your breath, but whatever you do, this approach will work better than trying to meet up with him or showing you're up for it.

At the moment he doesn't have feelings for you. The question of whether you can get him to have feelings for you – or, as I wanted, to leave the door open for future experimentation – is down to how much he cares about losing the flattery of your interest and how sexy he finds you when you're workin' it. Sad but true. However, my guess is that if he didn't think you were sexy enough when you first hooked up, he's not going to change that tune. As I say, steer clear of him.

3

Why does he go odd after a year, but won't end it?

THE STEVE FILES

It's one of the oldest jokes in the dating book: the guy begins to act so offish that eventually the mortified, mystified girl has no choice but to break it off. That it happens a lot, and that guys 'are afraid of women crying', is also old news. But the mystery remains: why? Why are so many adult males incapable of conducting a mature, honest break-up? Why is his fear so strong, he'll stay in something agonizingly awful for a year until finally the girl snaps? Why do they inflict Slow Death on a relationship when a short sharp break is evidently what they want? I remember my first boyfriend did this. I was thoroughly inexperienced and clung to what was becoming a total car crash thanks to him (and probably to me, in some way I had no idea about). He acted completely off with me, but let me continue to see him and to talk about us like we were together. Finally I couldn't take his unresponsiveness any more and I ended it. Me, the keeno who had been treated like a disease for weeks – I ended it. I wondered why it happened then, and I've wondered why it happens since – come to think of it, wasn't Christian (page 5) also a practitioner of Relationship Slow Death?

THE CASE

Alice and Steve, both teachers, were in the same crowd and had lots of friends in common, many of whom were shacked up with each other. Friends started saying they'd be great together, and one night – bam. They got together and within weeks were inseparable. At every opportunity with friends in the pub, Steve would rave about how in love he was. Alice had a permanent smile on her face. They'd talk about having babies together; Steve in particular seemed sold on the dream of the happy family and wanted it as soon as possible.

Their honeymoon phase lasted a year – every night spent together, each bringing the other books and music they'd like, going on adventures, and so on. But a year is a long honeymoon period for any couple, and eventually the magic stops coming by itself and you have to start making an effort.

Instead of ploughing forth, full of the joy of moving to the next, more realistic phase, Steve turned odd. He stopped caring as much as he'd done before; it started with little things like irritability and nonchalance. He wouldn't go to the pub with their friends, and when he did go, he'd ignore Alice. He'd moan about having to do things he'd have jumped to do before. She'd bring him books and he wouldn't open them. One night, when they were out at a bar with some friends who had been married for three years, Alice saw a scene of total adoration between the other couple when the girl went upstairs to find her husband, just to give him a quick hug. It made Alice burst into floods of tears: Steve hadn't touched her all night.

But Alice was in love with Steve, so despite being miserable she wanted to make it work. All the same, she couldn't help reacting to his coldness and bitchiness, so she stopped sleeping with him. They bickered and fought and were nasty to each other all the time by now, and didn't even have a sex life to make up for it.

He'd obviously developed some kind of phobia to her or the relationship, but wasn't prepared to end it. Finally, when it got so grisly there was no conversation left to have, Alice ended it.

She found out recently that he split up with his next girlfriend of two years, also having turned cold around the one-year mark, with her finally ending it. And, asking around, she found out he'd done the exact same thing with the girlfriend before her. One year gone, and suddenly the baby talk dies down, replaced by a disagreeable, awful new type of boyfriend, who drags the relationship down the drain slowly but surely.

What is going on with Steve? Had he just gone off Alice and found her a nuisance, along with the other two girlfriends? If that was the case, why be nasty to her instead of just ending it? Or was it just a childish anger at the reality of being in a relationship, namely that it takes work? Or is this the kind of guy who secretly itches to be polygamous and feels constrained in any relationship after a while?

WHAT THE GUYS THINK

BARRY M, 26, KING OF FLINGS

I've known Barry since school. He's a lovely guy so long as you're not his girlfriend or wishing you were (I never was or hoped to be). He's the king of going off women: I have seen him stop caring about whatever girlfriend he's with at about the one-year mark half a dozen times. He's perfect to comment on guys like Steve.

Make it deteriorate

'Obviously if you've been going out with a girl you like her, so you don't necessarily want to dump her and you don't want to hurt her.

So you just make the relationship deteriorate until she is forced to dump you. That way no one gets hurt. Straightforward, right?'

Yeah, if you're an idiot – or if you see things the way Barry and his ilk do. Why would acting like a Class A chump and therefore forcing her to end it hurt her less than coming clean? It's the difference between pressing an infected, putrifying bandage into a cut, or ripping it off quickly.

Bored

Now Barry gets nasty. But if that's how he's capable of thinking, I'm willing to believe it's how Steve, or guys acting like Steve, are thinking.

'He'd got bored of her, realized that all he ever did was flush his time down this sink that was their relationship, and wanted to maybe see his friends more and maybe twenty other hotter girls concurrently and have none of the lovey-dovey dependent book-club trash.'

This is almost unforgivably cruel. And while it's probably going too far, I'm afraid to say elements of it are probably true. That coldness (the ability to see the relationship/girlfriend as an unsexy time-drain) is something only a guy would be capable of.

So

Steve got bored and began to loathe the situation he found himself in. While he had failed to develop a sufficient bond with Alice to stave off this boredom, he also liked her, and their shared history made him reluctant to hurt her by dumping her. So he made her do it.

ROB Q, 27, SERIAL MONOGAMIST

I remember Rob before he was in his current relationship of six years. Despite being a total gentleman, he also left a bit of a trail of destruc-tion. That is, treating girls mean and coldly when he'd gone off them, only to make them swoon before finally ending it in tears.

Men are cowards

'Firstly, men are cowards. If we can avoid confrontation, and letting someone down, we will. That's why Steve's just acting out but not confronting Alice. Basically, Steve is finding he's beyond the exciting early stages of the relationship, and he's not taking it well. He seems to be having trouble accepting that things have to change with the passing of time. It's becoming increasingly obvious they are no longer in the first flush of love, and he needs to decide whether or not the relationship's worth pursuing at the expense of the independence he thinks he values. Of course, they've already kissed goodbye to independence by being in a relationship, but I bet he's been trying consciously or otherwise to avoid thinking about that fact.'

I'll say. The last thing it sounds like Steve's any good at doing is thinking intelligently about his relationships and emotions.

'This explains Steve's weirdness: the more Alice reacts to his odd behaviour, the more difficult he becomes as a confrontation with the reality comes closer. Personally, I tend to react in unpredictable and thoughtless ways when an assumption I've been making (in this case, that this is a new, carefree relationship) is exposed as no longer the reality.'

This is about guys trying to pretend reality isn't happening, because they've decided that it is all too scary, regardless of whether that is true.

So

Steve, ever the child, wants things easy and perfect all the time. He can handle the first year of relationships, because it's the easiest, most fun and most perfect. That the reality is ever so slightly less sexy when things get more serious is a major mental block for him. It's terrifying and awful and he doesn't want it because it reminds him of effort, entrapment, and so forth. So he throws his toys out the pram in the only way he can: he poisons the relationship, taking all his fear and loathing out on poor old Alice.

BOTTOM LINE

On the surface, Steve is just bored with the relationship (and always gets bored), which, coupled with his innate (Rob says cowardly) dislike of confrontation, means he puts off a break-up. This boredom, though, is likely part of a wider obsession with racking up the number of girls that are dependent on him, so that he feels validated and studly.

His cowardice has another form: the morbid fear of the realities of a longer-term relationship. Moving beyond the honeymoon phase terrifies him since it means he's one step closer to having his freedom curtailed, which would mean more compromise and less excitement. Wah! Must ruin!

Girls, think of it like this. The second he's acting shitty, he's trying to rip the plaster of the relationship off. You might as well do it yourself before it gets more infected – and, ultimately, more painful.

What to do if you want to save this: Barry has a fatalistic view, but Rob thinks there's hope for salvation. And since he's done what Steve's done before (albeit on a lesser scale), we should listen to him. 'In this kind of situation,' says Rob, 'a girlfriend can tap into a guy's mental block and coax him out of it by making him aware of what's really bothering him. Once they've honestly discussed it (and he's forced to stop playing games), they have a decent chance of moving on, since he'll realize things aren't as terrifying as he's making them out to be in his mind. He'll probably start off defensively when the topic gets discussed (anything to put off touching on the underlying truth), but if you can get him beyond that, there's hope.'

4

Why does he cheat on his new wife as though it's the most natural thing in the world?

THE DARREN FILES

You never have too many people on your side when you're complaining about being the other woman. You can barely get the words out before you're being accused of family-wrecking (though people seem to forget he's the one choosing to cheat). This is a typical sexist reaction: not to sound hackneyed and/or hairy 'n' angry, but a man who is seeing a married woman is considered a seducer of the highest order. There isn't even an equivalent male word for 'mistress', so I guess we'll have to stick with 'lover'. Certainly not 'master'.

I'm not advocating romances with married men, mainly because nothing very good is likely to come of it (and it's not very nice, especially if kids are involved). That said, true love is true love and people do leave their spouses for other people. But, generally, it's playing with fire. Perhaps not so much in an ancient, loveless marriage where both parties are at it. Recent figures suggest that half of married people will cheat at some point in their marriage, even in a happy one. But what's odd is how a lot of guys with young marriages mess around, as though it's just a bit of fun. They have no intention of leaving their wives, but equally seem uninterested in giving the marriage a chance. Somewhere down the line they just told themselves cheating was not only hunky-dory, but their marital right. What the hell are they thinking? (You might want to look at the quick-fire question on page 269 about why men really ask us to marry them. It's not always because they yearn to tie the knot, anyway.)

THE CASE

My friend Rosa is super-sweet and smart. Guys love her but they're usually not ones she loves back – nor does she date people until she's made sure she fancies them on several levels. This, along with having kept her head down all year (she's a trainee doctor), had landed her a bit of a dry spell.

Still, she wasn't particularly bothered about this – she had too much to do to spend time thinking about men or the lack thereof. But when Darren started working down the hall, she found herself distracted. The chemistry was amazing.

She knew he was married and didn't try to flirt, just enjoyed his company. But, within the confines of work and work socializing, Rosa was spending more and more time with Darren. He began making little moves and gestures – putting his hand on her knee, for example – when everyone was in the pub. She always pushed it away.

Nothing happened for ages. Rosa was appalled he was trying it on with her so persistently when he had a wife. And Rosa reckoned she wasn't the only one getting his attentions, though she was certainly his main interest.

One night she was so drunk and horny that she let Darren come up to her flat with her (he had texted his wife to say he was out drinking late with mates). They had a delicious shag, better for being forbidden and for being the result of months of pent-up desire. From then on they started having the affair Rosa had resisted. She was miserable about what she was doing, but she continued anyway. Soon enough he started saying he would leave his wife for her. By now Rosa was pretty smitten with him but wasn't sure she believed him.

Three months passed and the affair was getting more intense but also more complicated to maintain. She told him she wanted out. At this, he promised he'd tell his wife he was leaving her that very night.

The next day Rosa didn't hear from him. She hoped but somehow didn't quite believe he had done the deed. Sure enough, as he told her that night, he hadn't, but that was because his wife had had a cold. Rosa saw then that he had no intention of leaving her. He would have kept up the affair and promises for ever – that was probably his plan. She cut the cord and asked him to stop contacting her, which he did. She has since heard he's cheating with someone else now.

Why do the Darrens of the world give themselves the green light in the first place, and why do they bother with the old line about leaving their wives? Do they love their wives but find them dull? Do they love their mistresses but see them as eternal second fiddles from the get-go? Is it just that the girlfriend becomes less attractive when she becomes a wife?

WHAT THE GUYS THINK

PETER D, 29, IN A RELATIONSHIP

Peter has a literary mind that's cut out for the finest things in life. But he also understands the crude drives that motivate guys to risk all without properly risking it, if you know what I mean. In other words, the thrill of the new conquest, of fucking a newbie (see the Frank files for more on this, page 91), a woman who's not your wife.

Joy of transgression

'Darren enjoys having it both ways – his cake and eating it too. He wants the excitement of going after new women, the *newness*, the sizing her up, the potential, but doesn't really want to wreck his whole life up until that point.'

Hello, cake and eating it – men really like that.

'At times he thinks he will and does feel "true love" for Rosa, but that true love in the context of the affair has got to be so strong and so deep that if Darren did ever leave his wife it would have to be more than the simple allure of the other love. The marriage itself would have to be fundamentally broken up and dead. Darren would have to be pushed to the limit either at home by his wife in some way or by Rosa pressuring him. The reason for this is not because he doesn't love Rosa or see himself with her in the future, he simply likes the joy of transgression too much, the stepping outside of boundaries. It keeps him feeling like life is worth living, that there are things and experiences that he hasn't yet seen. He knows that if he simply leaves his wife for Rosa, Rosa will just become another wife.'

So

Why would you escape wife one for wife two? No, the man with a mistress needs both women: one to hold down the home front, his cosy, well-constructed life till now, and the other to provide the thrill of the new. He'll never leave one for the other. Unless of course his love for his mistress is one of those rare things, an absolutely all-consuming madness that usurps everything else, something so powerful he's willing to leave his fortress of domesticity 'fundamentally broken up and dead'.

GARY L, 28, LIVES WITH HIS GIRLFRIEND
Gary explains all of Darren's (and modern man's) temptations and relates to them. But ultimately he concludes that either you're the

kind of guy that gives in to temptation or you aren't. Marriage is merely a technicality when it comes to the resolve (not just the desire) to cheat.

Marriage is little more than a tax dodge

'The question here is not so much why do men cheat when they're in a marriage, as why do men cheat at all. Marriage these days has been massively devalued to the point where, in men's minds at least, it's little more than a tax dodge. Since so many people live together for a long period now before getting married, the key question is: does this man cheat on you while he's living with you? If the answer is yes, then that's not going to change after marriage.'

Morals v. dick

'One of the reasons cheating is so common these days is because of friendships like the one between Darren and Rosa. In ye olde tymes when men went to work and hung out almost exclusively with XY chromosomes, and women stayed at home, there was not much opportunity to forge friendships with the opposite sex. And friendships – acquaintances – have a way of leading to sex. Even if you feel there's one person you're in love with, there will always be chemistry with other people. It's difficult to predict which way a man is going to go: whether his morals are going to win, or his dick.'

So basically, just being out and about in the workplace and the normal modern world means you'll always be having chemistry here and there with whichever sexy flirty woman you are friends with. But big deal! I have chemistry with one of the builders I pass every day to work – it wouldn't make me cheat on a man for it. Saying no would be as hard as saying no to a nice piece of chocolate cake: difficult, but not *very* challenging.

Who I am

'I speak as someone who's been through Darren's temptations. Although I'm not married, I've been in a stable live-in relationship for some years, and as far as I'm concerned that's just as strong a commitment. Like Darren, and pretty much any modern man, I also have female friends and acquaintances who I socialize with, and I have chemistry with some of those. The chance to cheat is constantly available. And yet so far I've resisted it. Why? I honestly don't know. I could do all sorts of psycho-analysis, but the bottom line is: that's just who I am. And the bottom line for Darren (and a lot of other men) is: that's just who they are. I hate to sound priggish, but in the modern world for a man who's halfway presentable, *not* cheating takes a certain amount of self-discipline.

'Men do not see a distinction between long-term girlfriend and wife. If you've got a man who's justified (to himself anyway) cheating on you while you were his live-in girlfriend, then you're a fool to think he'll do any different when you're his wife. If you live together (hell, if you've been together six months) and he cheats on you, he's an adul-terer at heart. And that's simply what Darren is.'

Stop press. This strikes me as very important. Either he wants to be faithful to you or he doesn't – right from the get-go. It doesn't make any difference if you are married or not: a cheater is a cheater. We think twice *because* we're married. A lot of guys don't.

'And if he's got a woman who'll tolerate that, then of course he'll tell "the other woman" that he's going to leave when he has no intention of doing so: that's the ideal situation for such a man. Because deep down in their hearts, women know. Darren's wife knows, but she turns a blind eye. And that's the ideal wife for such men: she has a commitment to you; you have none to her. That's ultimately the life-partner Darren (and all such guys) are looking for: self-deceiving submissives. It doesn't sound like Rosa is such a woman. She's lucky to be out of it.'

Ba boom ching!

So

Gary nails it, and harshly too: a guy who cheats, no matter how early in the relationship, is an adulterer at heart. And only the most submissive, long-suffering type of woman would agree to be the wife of someone who sees no reason why he can't have his cake and eat it – his mistress and his wife. 'But what if she didn't know?' you ask. She knows. She's just turning a blind eye. Do you want to be that disrespected mouse? Do you hell.

BOTTOM LINE

This is not a man who has suddenly found himself in a sideshow he isn't sure how he got into. No, a guy like Darren wants both a wife and a mistress. His cosy wife holds down the fort at home, but she is boring and available – not in any way unnecessary, but, well, just his wife. How is he going to feel like a man again, to feel that thrill, the conquest of a woman who has no claims on him? Outside the marriage. But each woman is meaningless without the other. It's an endless interplay of the goddess and the whore. Except the mistress isn't limited to whore status. He may even love her and enjoy her intellectual charms. But it is unlikely that those feelings will get to the point where they require action on Darren's part, i.e. leaving his wife. He's got his life sewn up to a T and it's going to take a lot to break it up. You'll have heard the saying 'once a cheater, always a cheater'. Now you know why it's so damn true.

What to do if you're involved with a married man with Darren-esque traits: If he promises to leave his wife, don't hold your breath. In fact, exhale with an added gust of scorn at his feeble attempt to pull the wool over your eyes. Know this: you are in the compromised position, just like wifey. You provide the 'thrill' quotient on his list of must-haves, and that's it. What about your own list? If he ticks the same box for you – i.e. you're married or in a stable, unexciting relationship with a man, your job, whatever – then at least it's not unfair. But if you are cheating on your significant other with him, you're hardly heading down Good Karma Lane either. I know it's hard to end it with a charmer that you fancy and with whom you have good times and great sex, but if you let it go on too long, you'll find your life is passing by with nothing, lovewise, to show for it. If, however, you feel that something light and naughty is just what you want, and you're not developing expectations destined to be disappointed, then you should emerge unscathed, with only your conscience to deal with. One for the memoirs, anyway.

Quick-fire questions 1

What's the biggest thing a girl does that scares you/turns you off?

Now, ladies, pay attention here – this is a recurring theme. You have to stay cool. Hold something back even if you don't want to. Nothing is more offputting than depriving him of his chase. Common sense, really: the more it seems that you've got loads of options and don't need him to make you happy, the more he wants to be the only option. On the other hand, don't go over the top: seeming to follow a precise rule about not calling for three days is a turn-off.

MAX P: 'Being over-keen. The worst thing you can do is drunk-dial before your first date. This is not good. I once met a girl at a party, and we arranged to meet up, but then she called me at like 3 a.m. three days before, and basically was overexcited. I knew this was a bad sign. When we finally got to the restaurant I knew I wasn't keen, nor would I ever be.'

ALLEN P: 'What I really do not like at all is when people become unreasonably clingy and behave like they're scared stiff you're going to leave, since there's little that makes you more likely to do so. Someone I was seeing got really upset because I thought it was weird that she wanted to come with me to the hairdresser's. For no purpose other than just to Be Together At The Hairdresser's. At no point, even when entirely swaddled in fresh head-over-heels love, is that anything apart from irritating to me.'

MARIOS T: 'It probably has to be overenthusiasm about a relationship – plans being made too far into the future, mention of babies, etc. It is ironic because if a relationship is going well and the lady is enthusiastic then men lose interest, but if the lady is aloof then men are desperate to change this. Perhaps linked to this is that if someone becomes dependent on you (clinginess, for lack of a better word) it's an unattractive attribute, but independence is an attractive one.'

Do you tend to worry about girls getting too attached?

MARK C: 'Not really. I think it can be both a turn-on and a turn-off, depending on your thoughts about that person. If I'm unsure about how I feel about someone and they are super-keen it can be awkward and I usually end up feeling guilty. However, if I am really into someone then it can make everything super-special, for want of a better, more masculine phrase.'

JON D: 'The trouble with women is that it takes for ever to get one and for ever to lose one. Once you have got a woman in her comfort zone, she will not let the relationship go without a fight. So of course I worry about girls getting too attached. Girls always want to feel special. Guys do too, but not in the same way. But, if I want to be with her, she's worth every effort – every late-night cab ride over because she "wants to see me", every outing-when-all-you-want-to-do-is-stay-home. That said, the great girls make you not care. Maybe what I am trying to say is that sometimes as a guy you get taken for granted when she's too attached.'

Do I take guys for granted? Well, now that I think of it, I have been known to become furious if a man won't jump in the nearest taxi to come and meet me at a club because I am feeling horny and I want him there, regardless of whether he's loafing about at a mate's house on the other side of the city . . .

What do you think about public displays of affection and how soon do you go in for them?

KOBI N: 'I have no problem with public displays of affection after about one month, but only if I feel the relationship is a serious one.'

CHARLES S: 'I'm really funny about them – maybe that's just me being very British. I'm quite a private person and I don't like people speculating on my business. But once it's fully on and I'm really proud of it, then I think it's nice to be a bit physical – women like it, it makes them feel secure, and also a bit of you is proud and likes flaunting your "property", for want of a better word.'

What makes you class a woman as 'too needy'?

Neediness is a big thing women worry about being, and spend energy trying not to succumb to. At first I'm the most detached, the coolest of cucumbers, not a need in sight, and then, as soon as I feel he's *mine*, slowly it all falls away to reveal a needy madwoman.

THEO H: 'A person that needs constant attention, emotional support and personal affirmation, who phones more than three times a day to give and receive detailed life updates, who needs to be included in every decision, and is offended to be "left out" of anything, as well as simply easily offended, probably highly insecure, likely a jealous person, and suspicious of other women including friends and family; basically, high maintenance. This is unaccept-able because (a) it's tiring, and consumes so much unnecessary time and emotional energy; (b) I need the standard male minimum amount of personal space and time to myself – "Leave me alone; I have non-specific stuff to do!"; and (c) who would want to be with someone so insecure? The person I'm with must be emotionally self-sufficient, with her own life and interests, not depend-ent on me for everything, i.e. an adult. "Needy" people make you feel obliged to be with them – it's as if they're scared that if they're not on your case constantly you'll go off with someone else, which is an offensive implication in itself. But I don't want to feel obliged to be with someone, I want to feel like I have chosen to be with them.'

ROGER G: 'A needy girl is a dull girl, as she fixates more on the relationship than enjoying spending time with the other person in it.'

What is the most common excuse men use to keep things casual if they're not that into her?

ANTHONY A: 'Saying I just haven't got time for a proper girlfriend or I've only just come out of a relationship and just want to have some fun.'

STEVEN O: 'I'm very busy at work, or emotional turmoil.'

VICTOR L: 'If you're not that into her, you'll say, "I'm going out with the boys, come meet me afterwards", rather than "come with". It's a subtle booty call which is a big hint. If you're into her, you'd go for a drink with her first. Also, if the girl calls you but instead of answering you return with a text, that shows a lack of interest. For example, if a girl misses a call and replies with a text saying, "Hey, babe, sorry I missed your call, what's up?" I don't bother. Not being specific is a bad sign, you've got to pin down a date.'

Do you ever wish you were in a polygamous relationship?

MARK L: 'No. I'd be too worried that it would have to cut both ways, and she'd be polygamous as well, and I wouldn't want that. I can't imagine in any circumstances sharing a girlfriend with someone else. It would be horrible! It would destroy any kind of intimacy you had. And to be honest, I don't think I'd want more than one girlfriend. But if I could get rid of the moral qualms, I think it would be fun to have lots of different girls in a harem, like some Prince of Persia wannabe.'

ANTHONY S: 'I don't want to share my girl with anyone – and I don't want a girl who would be happy for me to have someone else in the relationship either.'

How do you react to a mate when he tells you he's cheated on his girlfriend?

VICTOR L: 'If it's an actual girlfriend, I'd be like, "Mate, that's a bit harsh", but I'd tell him not to let her know. I'd tell him he's got to end it but don't tell her – it would just cause needless hurt. My friends are good boys; if one of them did cheat, I'd lower my opinion of him.'

MAOR E: 'It depends. If I knew the girl well, and knew she was sweet and cute and really into him, I'd say, "Mate, sort it out, what are you doing?" Otherwise I probably wouldn't pass judgement; I may not even care that much.'

PART TWO

Sharing Space

*S*haring space is another of those issues that, although it affects both partners equally, usually leads to men becoming scared and jumpy and acting weird, while women are left wondering what the big deal is. See, it's a paradox: when we leave stuff at theirs, or want to move in with our man because he spends every night at ours anyway and it would just be easier, we get the blame for trying to thrust our lives on theirs and being over the top and outrageous and needy. Yet it's the guys who freak out and make a big deal out of it, not us. It's guys who invest stuff and space-sharing with so much fatal significance.

In fact, when it comes to space and stuff, usually we just want the practical solution with a dollop of affection ('Darling, can't you put your boxers somewhere that isn't my desk chair?'). Have you ever heard of a girlfriend who freaked because a guy left his razor or toothbrush at hers? I haven't.

So, over to you, boys. What's with the issues surrounding ownership of space? In this section we look at three different reactions to a woman making herself comfortable (or, in Justin's case, simply existing) in the same living space as her boyfriend.

One guy (Martin) had been seeing his sort-of girlfriend for three months when she accidentally left some jewellery by his sink. He went bananas (relatively speaking). She didn't even know what he was talking about at first. Another dude, Justin, acted like a real nut-job: he was a control-freak bachelor who couldn't handle the fact that when Lexie slept over, she would actually be there, with him, a real flesh-and-blood human. That he went ballistic at her for asking for a cuddle early in the morning was something so extraordinary I just had to turn it over to the guys to explain (and even they were a little taken aback).

And Ben. Well, this is a story a lot of women will relate to. He spent every night with his girlfriend but refused to move in with her. The idea of officially sharing a space with her – even though he was doing so unofficially anyway – was so morbidly terrifying to him that he couldn't contemplate it. If this isn't some huge imagined neurosis I don't know what is. How can living with the girlfriend you already practically live with be such a bad thing? Again, one for the guys – who, as predicted, have a lot of fear tied up with the moving-in question (as well as some suggestions on how you can get them through it).

In the Quick-fire section at the end, blokes reveal specifically what's so scary about moving in with us (newsflash: it isn't tampons), as well as who should do the cooking and whether snuggling in bed is actually a bit annoying. Mostly, the answers aren't as bad as you might fear; a lot sound terrifyingly reasonable. Almost, dare I say it, something we might have thought ourselves.

5

Why is he an arsehole during sleepovers when you're still in the honeymoon phase?

THE JUSTIN FILES

Normally the honeymoon phase lasts for three months and, quite often, longer. This is your 'anything-goes' time – no fights develop because nothing is annoying. You demand he rushes to your place at 2 a.m. because you feel like a kiss? Oh, how adorable, he'll be right there. He wants to stay up all night looking at the stars on a school night? How romantic! You fancy a *Sex and the City* marathon *à deux*? Done.

But what's going on when a honeymoon phase is marred by weird outbreaks of anger, the type you might expect to see two years down the line? This case is about a guy who showed plenty of promise of being a keen-bean future boyfriend, but who was simply unable to tolerate the situation he also seemed to want. Nothing riled him more than his new girl's presence at his place overnight.

I think this anger is worth investigating, because anger and irritability are hard to reverse in relationships that have gone on for a while, and are particularly problematic when they arise in men, who repress more thoughts and feelings than we do. This makes it harder – as a woman – to understand the problem, work on it and move on. Justin is an interesting case because his anger and irritability were so naked and seemingly out of the blue. If we can understand why he acted like he did, it might shed light on other more common forms of hostility. Plus, it's a good excuse to learn what guys really think about bed-sharing and cuddling.

THE CASE

My friend Lexie, who lives in LA, was really excited about meeting Justin, having been through enough duds lately. He was perfect: super-affectionate and admirably moral (he worked for a charity that helps orphans). He was 34 and had been single for ages.

When they met up it was brilliant, but he often seemed nervous about sacrificing his friends and other commitments in order to see her, so they didn't meet as much as she'd have liked. Nevertheless, Lexie made a huge effort to respect his need for space because she thought he was great and they had a lot in common. Her patience seemed to be paying off – their relationship was growing and he was getting more attached, wanting to see her more.

Things went horribly wrong a month into it. Lexie, who lived on the other side of town from him, had to be in his neck of the woods for a work-related outing that involved an evening and an early morning. She asked if he wanted to meet up, suggesting perhaps she could spend the night. He said yes, it would be nice to see her.

She went round, they had a nice evening, including good sex, and then it was time for bed. Lexie snuggled down, but Justin began playing his guitar. This caused some tension, as she suggested as gently as possible that it was probably time to sleep – she'd love to hear him at some point, just not now when they had to get up early. He was a bit grumpy, but got into bed.

He then popped an Ambien, a sleeping pill popular in the States, which provides seven hours of uninterrupted sleep. Slightly surprised at the froideur of the pill-popping, it was only when he refused to cuddle her that Lexie started to suspect something was up. Maybe they weren't at the impromptu sleepover stage after all. But she couldn't sleep with such hostility, and finally, at 6.30, woke him to say she couldn't sleep, hoping for some reassurance.

Rather than 'poor baby, have a snuggle', his reaction was rage. 'I cannot believe you just woke me up,' he snarled, and seemed truly cross. Lexie was shocked, and tried to apologize, but he didn't melt. He jumped out of bed, forced her to get up too and practically shoved her out the door with him at 7.20 a.m., an hour before she needed to leave. As they parted ways, he told her that he knew it was a mistake letting her come round on a week night, and that he couldn't believe she'd messed up his whole day by waking him up too early, probably before the sleeping pill had worn off.

An hour later he sent an email saying that since they obviously couldn't meet up any more on weekdays, that left them with weekends, which weren't much easier in the coming weeks because of various events he had to go to. It was over.

How could Lexie have ruined everything with one ill-judged wake-up call? Had he sensed she was asking something of him, something more than he was ready to give? Lexie said his grievance seemed to stem from her interfering with his ability to work. But what possessed him? Is that what being a confirmed bachelor leads to?

WHAT THE GUYS THINK

TOM L, 28, RECENTLY SINGLE

Tom is the nicest guy in the world, and had an enviable relationship with his most recent girlfriend. Their break-up still saddens me. They lived together and slept together harmoniously for several years in a tiny flat. Even so, he's sensitive to the things that can disrupt a guy's sleep, and annoy less patient dudes more than we might have ever imagined, especially bachelors. Men and their routines. Remember your dad, the toilet and the newspaper? Every day after breakfast? Same idea.

Time-honoured routine

'Yes, he sounds like a total dickhead. But sleep patterns are an extremely personal thing. I don't know if it's just a guy hang-up, but the slightest change can really throw you off, especially if you're a hardened bachelor with a time-honoured routine. Now, Justin clearly winds down by strumming his guitar at night. People just have their things. It may well also be that either the sleeping pill is a normal part of his routine, or, having had his routine knocked off, and finding sleep flitting away, he decided to go with the pill to fit in with Lexie, rather than being some passive-aggressive move to upset her.'

If this was his attempt to accommodate Lexie, then one thing's for sure: you can never tell what lurks beneath the surface.

Ten wrong ways to cuddle

Tom gets technical here. But there's nothing like cold hard facts.

'Cuddling can throw you off your sleep,' he says. 'It can indeed be very relaxing for the guy, but it has to be the right way – there are ten wrong ways to cuddle compared to one right way. For instance, the girl might be spooning you, breathing on your neck, which will for some reason become super-sensitive, leaving you hyper-aware of this irritation and unable to sleep. Similarly, you may be spooning her, only to find you've got a dead arm. Or if you're lying on your back and she's cuddled into you with her head on your chest and/or shoulders, there's a surprising array of pressure points where it's really uncomfortable to have your partner's head, and where it can really interfere with your sleep. So don't take the non-cuddling thing too personally. Even though this guy was a total douchebag about not even attempting to explain himself, I can understand where he's coming from.'

So

Lexie pushed all his well-settled bachelor buttons. By disrupting his sleep and unsettling his routine, she was making the realities of what it is to be in a relationship crashingly clear to him – and he couldn't hack it all at once. Suddenly, in his mind's eye, he saw his whole carefully built world crash down and his reaction was classic panic. With long-term bachelors, you can never give them enough time to adjust.

DAVE B, 27, IN A SERIOUS RELATIONSHIP
Dave has had a lot of girlfriend experience and he is very clear-headed about relationships. He has little time for the likes of Justin, bachelor or no.

Not happy with himself

'The guy is a weirdo. That's why he's good-looking, successful, 34 and single. If you scream at someone in the first month of knowing them, something's seriously off. The fact that he's taking sleeping pills means he can't lie in a room on his own in the dark without getting agitated, nervous and filled with thoughts and regret. He's not happy with himself.

   'What she should do is first of all have confidence she's not to blame; it seems she's asking herself if she did something wrong, which is misguided. You have to know what's right or wrong. It takes practice in relationships to know when to turn around and say, "That was psychotic behaviour and I'm not interested." Yet that is exactly what needs to be done in this situation.'

So

Settled bachelor or no, Justin's flare of temper was grounds for dismissal because if he's like that in the early days, imagine what will come next:

hissy fits because she didn't chop the onions small enough, a walkout because she is late home from work one day.

That he had such issues around sleep shows that he has an unsettled mind. Until he gets a grip on that, he's not going to get a grip on the temper and probably won't be boyfriend material.

BOTTOM LINE

If Lexie was really willing to give him a go, she would have to take things even more slowly with Justin, to give him extra time to adjust and be 'trained' to share things – like his bed – with her. But it's a long shot. The temper tantrum would imply that he's not worth salvaging and has gone too far down the control-freak bachelor path. The tantrum and the sleeping pills would imply that, contrary to appearances, he's rather on edge, and may well need therapy to get to the bottom of it all. It could take a lot of treatment to resolve the anger and, until then, he's not in a fit state to be the boyfriend of someone who likes a cuddle when she can't sleep.

What to do if, for some weird reason, you still want to make this work: Be on bachelor alert and allow him plenty of time to adjust to new sleeping arrangements on Friday and Saturday nights. 'Men are trainable like dogs, but they aren't as smart, and don't learn new tricks so quickly,' says Tom. Be extra sensitive to their bedtime rituals in case they're too embarrassed to spell out their importance. Who knows, maybe Justin's pill-popping grump started when Lexie failed to dig the pre-bed strumming.

6

Why does he spend every night at yours, but refuse to move in?

THE BEN FILES

On the scale of commitment, moving in together does rank rather high. Still, the arrangement can be terminated at any time, easy-peasy. It's nothing like as scary as marriage and babies.

Relationships develop, and if they don't, then you've got to wonder why you're bothering. Of course, if one person really isn't up for it, if they like spending (or need to spend) a few nights a week on their own, for example, then maybe it's not the right thing and possibly won't ever be. But what is it with guys who spend every single night at their girlfriend's flat, but get all funny about moving in? (By all funny, I mean they refuse to let it happen.)

This has happened to several friends of mine in long-term relationships. They spend every night with their significant other, they're getting on for 30, and – when the moving-in option finally becomes so glaringly obvious it has to be dealt with – their boyfriends either come up with some ridiculous excuse or run a mile. What gives?

THE CASE

My friend Julia, 28, had been going out with Ben, also 28, for two years; she is in her final year of medical school (having come to it late) and he works for a charity. They became intense quickly, and he was the sort of guy to send her roses at random, and plan original ways to surprise her on Valentine's Day and at Christmas.

Things progressed nicely: they went on holiday together and with each other's parents. They became part of each other's families. By about the one-year mark, despite having busy individual social lives, they were spending almost every night at either his or her flat – usually his, since she had three flatmates and lived in west London, whereas he had his own flat in central London (which was more convenient for work).

They had been together for eighteen months when Julia's landlord decided to sell the house in west London; she and her flatmates had to leave. Julia was quite pleased, because it was the perfect time to take the obvious next step of moving in with Ben. She almost didn't feel the need to discuss this at length with him, it seemed so natural. So she was more than slightly thrown when he said, 'Sure, baby, live with me until you find a new place.'

Still, she went along with this, believing it was just something he'd said because he hadn't given much thought to them living together, inertia being the powerful force that it is. Plus, she figured if he was a little wary of it, this would be a good test and opportunity for both of them to try it out. So she moved in 'temporarily'. It was bliss; they had the perfect balance between his and her social lives and time together. Neither was too messy or inconsiderate. It was just so much easier than having some stuff here and some stuff there. Julia's joy at being able to access most of her wardrobe in the morning was sizeable.

But towards the end of about three weeks, Ben raised the prospect of Julia's flat-hunt. He still didn't want to live with her, and was expecting her to find somewhere else. He said some things about not being ready, and the personal space issue, but it all rang false, since they had got on so well during the weeks Julia had been there. Sure, her stuff might have been more present than he liked, but that was because she hadn't unpacked properly, not having been invited to stay.

So Julia moved out, and they stayed together for another few months. But Julia couldn't forgive him, or understand his reluctance to move in with her. The relationship unravelled. Since then he's been in touch to say that he misses her and wants her back – but he still hasn't addressed the issue of why he is so against cohabiting.

Now, Julia wasn't hell-bent on marriage and babies with Ben. But she wanted to see if it was a possibility, and living together not only seemed like the enjoyable next step, but would make their lives easier, not harder. So why did Ben resist, when he'd been such a devoted boyfriend for all that time before? Why was he happy spending every night with Julia, but so resistant to her moving in, even for an indefinite trial period? Was he just scared it would all lead to marriage too soon? Did he have doubts about Julia? Was he making a final plea for independence, and, if so, why was he bothering to keep the relationship so strong?

WHAT THE GUYS THINK

JOHNNIE M, 29, IN A RELATIONSHIP

Johnnie is a clever guy who is a romantic and tends to have intense relationships, but likes to play the field. He's still hung up on freedom, and has not yet been tempted by the idea of moving in with a woman. He understands where Ben is coming from all too well.

The issue, as Johnnie perceives it, is about being invaded, smothered and doomed to this fate for ever, the bachelor-pad dream dead as a dodo, which many men see as a tragedy in and of itself. That said, can the relationship be so great if the idea of living together is so unpalatable? Johnnie hints perhaps not.

Already feel the faultlines

'Moving in together is a terrifying idea. It's the end of the possibility of just having your own space without needing a reason for it, just as I've always slightly lamented that moment when you come to need a specific reason not to see the other person, rather than a specific reason to do so. That's why I've always been nervous about being around each other all the time.'

Yes, but presumably you're with someone who respects your space. And when you live together you can both be out in the evenings doing your own thing, safe in the knowledge you can kiss each other good night or good morning. It's not about 'being around each other all the time'. But men, as we know, are super-sensitive about anything that could spell constraint.

'I've personally never lived with a girlfriend, but it's come up twice, and in both cases I sort of batted it away, not because the prospect wasn't actually very nice, but because I could already feel the faultlines in the relationship that would inevitably lead to fractures. And I think you can see someone pretty seriously and legitimately say you love them while at the same time knowing that living together is a different thing. I just couldn't get the idea out of my head that at some point one of us would be leaving the place alone, and that made me too sad to countenance being reminded of on a daily basis.'

This is evidence of my hunch that there is more depth behind guys' actions than you'd ever think. They see potential problems that may only develop over years and only when cohabiting. This worries them because they don't want conflict, hurt or trouble, especially when they can avoid it. And this vision of leaving alone, which several guys have shared with me, is another one you wouldn't see coming. The drama of our male friends can be staggering.

So

When a guy is weird about moving in, it's because he's already imagined the end of the relationship is up ahead. That doesn't mean it is, or that he doesn't love you, but it does mean that it's not perfect and that if you become any more present in his life, he might suffocate. That means you'll have to wait until his fears of suffocation settle (if you can be arsed) – and until he realizes that although you're not perfect, nobody is. Better yet, show him where he's going wrong by saying you understand his issue but you won't hang around for ever. More on this theme later.

ANDY B, 45, MARRIED

I asked Andy to comment after his wife told me over lunch that it had been nigh on impossible to get him to move in with her. She said he and his mates felt the same way about living with a girlfriend, but that he was the worst. Nevertheless, in the end, obviously, he went for it. See? It can work out.

Jumping off a cliff

'I recognize me and lots of other men in Ben. You may ask what the difference between moving in and staying over all the time really is. But psychologically for men, there's a huge difference. In men's minds, that little step is a huge step. Not only does it represent the giving up of your independence, it's about giving up the end of your youth as well. Guys think, "Regardless of what age I am, mentally, my youth is now gone." You're no longer a lad any more. Of course the reality is that nothing changes anyway: you only give up your independence if you want to.

'Me and friends used to talk about it; we literally used to see it as jumping off a cliff. About holding your nose and closing your eyes and jumping. In actual fact, instead of plummeting, and falling and falling, you just drop a centimetre.'

Women make life too easy for blokes

Ladies, we're hearing it again and again. We have to toughen up. We've become too meek.

'Women have made life too easy for blokes,' says Andy. 'Now, blokes can have their cake and eat it. People date for years without moving it beyond. They've got the nice cosy domesticity on one hand, but it's not really a permanent situation. It's not secure for the woman as the guy doesn't have to promise anything. This is unfair.'

OK, it sounds a little old-fashioned. 'We don't need promises and security!' you rage. But, well, we do want to feel settled when the time is right. Basically, there comes a point when we're tired of waging a war on the male fear of long-term commitment.

Andy puts it bluntly: 'Women should be harsher and give more ultimatums. Ben would be crying into his beer if Julia just said, "You know what? I'm done, I'm out." If women did that more, I guarantee blokes would change their ways. Women have made it incredibly easy for us. I know guys who have been going out with women for seven, eight years but are not committing to a longer-term relationship. Women want to settle down, especially when they want to have kids. Blokes are happy just to roll along.'

So

If you want to settle down, you have to be tough with the guy and not compromise. Tell him you're out if he doesn't play ball. If Julia had used this tactic on Ben, he'd almost certainly have changed his tune and they may well have moved in together instead of spending months in a wishy-washy limbo.

ROB D, 29, IN A RELATIONSHIP

Rob is a very sensitive, mature guy. He recently came out of a long-term cohabiting relationship. He knows all about the perils of moving in – and out. Like Johnnie, he says the main issue with Ben is doubt that Julia isn't quite the woman he wants to jump off the cliff for.

Waiting for a sign

'Ben resisted moving in with Julia because he was waiting for a clear sign that she was the right one. Even though all the right things were in place and they were happily coasting along as the perfect couple, Ben still didn't feel like he was *absolutely* sure she was the woman worth giving up his independence for. He loved spending every night with Julia, but secretly, when they were apart and he had a night alone, he would breathe deeply and relish the fact that he was free, that he still had a get-out-of-jail card. Ben was waiting for a sign that Julia was *it*, even if he didn't know what the sign would look like.'

Would a pig flying be it, perhaps?

Forced into a corner

'The problem for Ben was also that Julia's circumstances had forced him into a corner where he wasn't in control of the situation. The idea of moving in together may have been fine as a distant prospect, but one that in Ben's mind would come about at a time of his choosing, and on his terms. Julia being kicked out of her flat meant that suddenly he was expected to do something that he hadn't initiated. It was basically a control thing.'

That old control thing again. The second the man isn't calling the shots, be it with texting between the first few dates or choosing when to call it a 'relationship', he starts to lose it.

So

Suddenly the power dynamic established in the beginning when Ben won over Julia was upended, and therefore put the basis of the relationship into question. Ben freaked as soon as an event forced the relationship into a realm outside of his exact control. Maybe he wouldn't have worried about control so much if he hadn't also been worrying that Julia wasn't the one. Where's a sign from God when you need one, eh?

BOTTOM LINE

In general, men do not like the prospect of moving in with their girlfriends. It signals the end of freedom and youth and destroys their idea of their potency. It also makes them think they might be smothered without hope of having their own space ever again. It's all fear and rubbish, but it's certainly there. Nevertheless, a word of warning: when a guy is reluctant to move in, don't just assume it's about freedom entirely. Two out of three guys here say it's about doubts. If he's having doubts about you, the relationship is probably due a nice long discussion.

What to do if you still love him badly and want to make it work: There are two options for women caught in Julia-like situations. One option is to bring the underlying problems to the surface. This isn't straightforward. 'If the relationship is not at a stage where the girlfriend is able to understand the weirdness and talk to the boyfriend about it,' says a male friend, 'then there is little hope. Once he's reacted to something by freaking out, either he'll need careful coaxing to accept that there's something going on that he hasn't thought about, or he'll get increasingly defensive and impossible to talk to as he tries to stick with his original nonsensical position.'

If she succeeds, and he is able to admit there's a hidden fear here, they may well move beyond it, in the same way a zit will heal once you've popped it.

The other option is scarier but *far* more effective as well as admirable: the ultimatum. Don't want to move in with me? Forget the whole thing then, pal. As Andy says, he won't know what to do with himself and next thing you know, he'll be begging to sign on the dotted line.

7

Why does he freak out when you leave something at his?

THE MARTIN FILES

Often, in the early stages of a relationship, men will be extra sensitive about things that smack of greater commitment than they feel ready for. This is fine, if those sensitivities are grounded in reality. Showing your boyfriend a pregnancy book 'just for fun' after four months would send any man into an 'I'm not ready for that' terror.

What's odd is when a guy freaks out at some perceived trespass on his personal space, or some alleged advancement into serious-ville, when it's something you think is minor and no big deal. Why would leaving a few bits and bobs of your stuff at his send him into a tailspin? Remember that episode in *Sex and the City* when Carrie rejoices because Big has allowed her to keep a toothbrush at his, even though they've been together for months? Weird. And why?

THE CASE

My friend Mary met her then-boyfriend Martin at a pub quiz night. He is a serious guy, not particularly up for games and frivolity, and this was reflected in his instant fascination with Mary, who is very driven and committed to her work in education policy and who has a taste for gritty thrillers that Martin shared.

He wooed her heavily, taking her on trips to the theatre, cooking dinner for her, and so on. He was great, but not an overly straightforward guy. He'd hinted at recent personal grief without talking much about it, and had once been engaged to someone but had broken it off. I remember Mary saying she couldn't always read him and sometimes he seemed to have a shadowy side that he hid.

A few months into this burgeoning relationship, Mary slipped up without realizing it. Staying at his as she normally did, Mary left her bracelets and watch in the bathroom by the washbasin.

Next time she came round, two days later, he was all funny with her. Then he said with a grim expression that she couldn't leave her stuff around like that; it wasn't fair to his flatmates. He seemed really irritated and shaken and she apologized, telling him the truth, which was that she had done it without thinking and couldn't see what the fuss was about. They stayed together for another two months but then things went pear-shaped and he said family issues were distracting him. He basically did everything to end it without actually ending it (see the Steve Files in Chapter 3): he was cold, snappish and remote. She never questioned him directly about the bracelets incident, having sort of forgotten it in the mess of everything else. But after they broke up and she thought about it all, she couldn't help but date the beginning of the end of the relationship back to that occasion. That was the first time he ever acted oddly and as anything other than the devoted suitor. It only got worse from that moment.

What is it about men, stuff and weirdness? Apparently Mary had violated some boundary by leaving her bracelets by his washbasin, even though they had been together for three months at the time. What was Martin afraid of – his flatmates thinking Mary was moving in? Mary becoming too big a part of his life? Why do men invest our stuff with such significance?

WHAT THE GUYS THINK

JARL L, 31, IN A LONG-TERM RELATIONSHIP

Jarl is a pretty straight-down-the-line type of guy, and I can't for a minute imagine him making a fuss about some bracelets here or there. But what he does recognize in Martin's behaviour isn't just fear of stuff. Jarl thinks it's a way (albeit a childish one) of saying 'hang on a minute' to the relationship.

Doesn't want to show other people

'He wasn't interested in her in a serious way. He has an issue, and it's either that he doesn't really see her as his girlfriend or he's got a phobia of relationship advancement.'

OK, do you see how Jarl put it, 'doesn't really see her as his girl-friend'? That is a huge thing with guys, and often determines whether something ever progresses beyond casual dating or even just fuck-buddying. They have to envision us as girlfriends in the early days, before we become girlfriends. They have ideas about how their girl-friends are meant to be, in their mind's eye. If they don't see us that way, we don't have a chance. It's a bizarrely rigid outlook, but it comes up again and again. Anyway, back to Jarl.

'The former is most likely (i.e. not seeing her as a girlfriend) and his weirdness about the bracelets is a sign that he doesn't want to show other people that it's serious. When a woman leaves things at yours it's a sign of getting comfortable in your space.'

And that she'll be hard to get rid of – a bit like mice.

'If you didn't want that to happen, you might react as Martin did. Sounds to me like he didn't feel able to articulate where his reaction came from so he just acted out instead of talking to her about where they were going.'

So

Because Martin was not serious about a future with Mary, he was hyper-sensitive to any signs that she was under a different impression. We all know how much men hate the guilt of leading women up the garden path and how childishly they deal with it (recall Jeremy in Chapter 2). Add to that the disproportionate fear of what will happen when a woman moves in (even if it's likely to be miles down the line), and you've got Martin freaking out at a few bracelets by the washbasin.

ILDUT L, 29, SINGLE

Ildut is French, and gives a great deal of thought to women. He's hyper-sensitive to turn-offs and turn-ons. Like so many guys, signs of attachment from the right woman are welcomed and encouraged, and from the 'wrong' one, reviled.

Precursors to a lot more

'I wouldn't mind if my girlfriend, who stays at mine regularly, leaves in my room a toothbrush, contact lenses liquid or even a spare pair of pants for practical reasons (a girl will stay more easily at yours if she has her minimum comforts). But these are all pretty functional items. Leaving bracelets and so forth serves no such purpose, so I can see how Martin may have seen them as the precursors to leaving a lot more, and then, basically, her moving in. He was clearly not thinking seriously about a future with Mary if the very idea of her moving in made him go off the wall. I'd be the same – it's significant enough when a girl leaves her lenses. Her jewellery is another matter and it belongs in her jewellery box, at home. This is how a guy could see it, even though from Mary's perspective it might have been just a thoughtless act.'

So

Men have specific ideas about what constitutes reasonable or appropriate items to leave at their place: toothbrush, eye stuff and pants are all OK. Anything more than what is strictly necessary reminds them of a future they don't yet want and perhaps will never want – with you. Then they freak. Ahh.

BOTTOM LINE

Men invest stuff with importance only if they are uneasy about the relationship getting serious. This anxiety arises because either they're not keen enough or they're generally used to panicking at the idea of commitment and it's become a pattern. Above all, it's a sign that you're getting comfortable in his space, quite possibly before he wants you to. Despite Martin's apparent keenness, he obviously wanted things to move at a snail's pace and on his terms.

What to do if you want to save your relationship: Another friend I asked about this puts it well: 'The thing to do with a guy like this is take a big step back. Wait for him to suggest staying over; don't just come round and assume it's all right. As a man, you don't really want the girl to tell you she's staying; you want it to be the other way round, her prize for being great.'

   Ladies, we may choose to think of it differently: as his prize for being great. Either way, we're playing games here with a guy like Martin, and unless you play well, game over.

Quick-fire questions 2

What's so scary about moving in with someone?

Here it is spelled out: most guys immediately see it as the death of freedom. Cosy, convenient domesticity – what we tend to relish – is something that they want only much later in life.

JAMES E: 'Moving in together feels like an all-to-play-for move. If you've ever had to move out of a place you've shared with a girlfriend, you know that it feels like "My Little Divorce". Moving in is a huge step. It means this relationship goes one way or the other: it ends happily with marriage or long-term commitment, or it's going to be hard to extricate oneself from.'

ALEK B: 'The main fear is of ending up living with someone who needs company all the time and thereby makes you a miserable wreck with no freedom. I've made that mistake before, when I was married, and I'm now careful not to develop a relationship with someone who can't be comfortable with time alone. Knowing when to give the other person space and how to do it is mandatory for living together, otherwise it's awful. I think a lot of guys worry that their girlfriend might end up being more needy/ demanding than is healthy.'

Does it annoy you when a girl leaves her things at yours?

MARK M: 'I don't mind a girl leaving things at mine, but it depends of course on how I feel about her, and what it is. One of my bedside cabinets is always free for a girl to put some stuff in.'

ED H: 'I think it shows some maturity and belief in the relationship if you can leave some overnight clothes, a fresh shirt, a toothbrush or some deodorant at someone's place. No need to go overboard though.'

NICK H: 'Small things, like girl clutter, are indicative of the bigger things. If a girl leaves her stuff at mine, and the basic example of her existence irritates me, then there might be a problem that goes slightly deeper than keeping my room tidy (never a priority at the best of times). The first poem I wrote was about the paraphernalia of a girl at uni and how every ring or strand of hair made me ache with love and reverence – but that's because I loved her.'

Is there anything that grosses you out, like tampons or stray dirty knickers?

KOBI N: 'Nope, I'm not grossed out easily, but I would prefer not to be exposed to tampons if not necessary.'

SCOTT M: 'Not really, I'm pretty tolerant of bodily fluids, and used to dirty washing. It's just a fact of life, and one should be careful not to judge too much, lest your own disgusting habits are suddenly not tolerated. And I know there are plenty of those. However, most people keep that stuff under control.'

Do you sleep better sharing your bed with a woman?

CHRIS R: 'It is definitely more comfortable to have more space in bed. Sometimes I have to work abroad or away, and therefore I stay in hotels. Often the bed is big, comfy and full of pillows. I have to admit I do sleep very well, and it's nice to stretch out, but in those moments when you're falling asleep, and similarly in those moments when you stir in the morning, it is my wife that I miss.'

NICK H: 'I sleep better after sex, and that generally involves a girl, but then I sleep better after a day's cycling, so I think that's down to endorphins. If you're in love with your bedfellow, then it seems that your bodies tend to snake round each other in more of a glove-fit, and waking up can be sensational.'

Do you ever find her desire to snuggle annoying?

PETE R: 'Yes. There are two examples when this annoys me. One: I am tired and trying to get to sleep. I can't get to sleep facing her with her arm over my face, because a) it's too hot and sweaty, and b) the air is recirculating from my mouth, bouncing off her arm and then back into my nose. I'm not great at physically sleeping with other people though. Two: sometimes (not always) after having sex, particularly in the morning, this might be bad, but I quite often want to get a glass of water or walk around a bit immediately afterwards to stretch my legs – yes, it does sound terrible – but instead I'm stuck there for twenty minutes.'

What's your attitude towards cooking when you live together – take it in turns or the woman's job?

MOSHE B: 'I do a lot of the cooking, but I like my cooking. We don't really take it in turns; it's more whoever can be arsed to do it. But in a fantasy world I love the idea of being cooked for and looked after. I think most men, when they get married, remember their earliest relationship with a woman – their mum – so you want to be taken care of, you want to be mothered by your wife. Guys love to be cooked for. But these days, it's about who can be arsed.'

SUBO W: 'Usually I'm a much better cook than my girlfriends, so I nearly always cook.'

LOU A: 'I love cooking so I am happy to do most of it. I don't see it as a woman's job at all, in fact most of the men I know (around the late twenties, early thirties mark) all really enjoy cooking and take great pride in making something that their partners and friends enjoy. It's sickening in a way, because it means that as we get older we get closer to those vomit-inducing scenes at the end of the original *Naked Chef*, when Jamie would be joined by "friends" for a sort of middle-class dinner-party dream sequence.'

How important is neatness to you? Would a slovenly living partner turn you right off?

MARK F: 'Yes, I would be quite put off by a slovenly living partner. Not least because I'd always feel the need to tidy up after them.'

WILL S: 'I remember a girl at university who I shared a house with. One day we went into her room, and after struggling to get the door open we were greeted with more dirty knickers than you could shake a stick at, tampons, ear buds, bras, papers, lots of old plates and cups . . . just everything you could ever imagine. There was no sign of the carpet. Frankly it was fucking disgusting, and she should have been ashamed of herself. Away from her parents, shut behind her door, she had simply gone feral. Not cool. As long as you aren't like that then you're OK in my eyes.'

PART THREE

Mixed Signals

It used to drive me crazy. For a very long patch, every time I started seeing a guy, it would only be a matter of time until he threw us off course. He'd be super-keen and gung-ho for the first few dates, then go out of touch, only to reappear a week later as if nothing odd had happened. Or he'd make it obvious he was enjoying our time together as much as me (and more, if the vigorous and sometimes premature groping was anything to go by), then go off the radar between meetings, leaving me hanging. Or, better yet, he'd tell me he wasn't really up for it, then keep calling for chats or to suggest meeting up seemingly as friends.

I got dizzy trying to work out what these guys were thinking, what those signals meant, and whether I should persevere and wait around for the penny to drop about how badly they wanted me. (I'm one of those girls who usually can't help letting things go on unsatisfactorily even though I know I'm on the receiving end of something a bit rubbish.)

Mixed signals are what keep us sitting round for hours with our girlfriends downing bottles of wine or necking mojitos and trying to work out what the hell is going on. How he was nuzzling your neck and cooing, post-coitally, about how amazing it feels being with you – and yet, three days later, you've heard nothing from him. Or how he's told you he's not interested but then tried to hold your hand when you ran into each other in the pub.

Few men are straight-shooters, and a lot of the time they'll start something for one reason (the chance to have a shag) and then panic when they also seem to be 'seeing' the shagee. That's one answer; it could be any number of other reasons. Which is why dating can feel like navigating an impossible labyrinth.

I had to choose some specific mixed-signal stories, so I went for those closest to my and my friends' hearts. Alan is a good one: he acted all entitled and boyfriendy (DVDs and red wine on the sofa on a Friday night, hello!), but was he really up for being my boyfriend? It didn't seem like it – and all the guys I asked about it said no way, in the form of various harsh truths.

Jim is another classic. He embodies that thing that guys do where they dismiss you as a girlfriend but keep you on as a friend type, even though that's clearly not what either of you is looking for. What kind of friend are you meant to be? The possible fuck-buddy, the possible distant-future girlfriend or a doting admirer to flatter his ego?

Then there's Frank: enormous gestures and extravagant wooing – those, in fact, of a man in love – before disappearing off the face of the earth.

And Mark, who stays in a relationship he's clearly not enjoying and has already poisoned when he obviously wants out.

The topic is endless, but should seem less scary and incomprehensible when you've read what my men have to say. Perhaps more than in any other section, we see all the complex reasons guys keep us around when they aren't sure we're for them or even know we're not. In the Quick-fire section, you'll find out exactly why guys string us along, as well as whether they also agonize over when to send texts. Sometimes, after all, sending mixed signals is a way of playing it cool. Which is a way of showing you care. Arrrghh.

8

Why does he act like a boyfriend when you're physically together, but go quiet when you're not?

THE ALAN FILES

Like any girl who's lived unhitched in a big city for a while, I don't expect every dalliance to turn into a committed relationship. Who would want that anyway? It's all about trying things out and not stopping – for long, anyway – until you find something awesome. Forcing things to be more than they are, or should be, is exhausting and never works.

Of course, casual dating's no piece of cake. It's rather an art to stay happy in its odd, limbo-ish confines.

The key, though, is to identify quickly the nature of your liaison and adjust your expectations and behaviour accordingly. If it's casual, i.e. you see each other unpredictably and the intimacy is sporadic and circumstantial, recognize this fact and take it or leave it. Which is exactly what I was trying to do while dating Alan, a whimsical musician type who was 'into film'.

THE CASE

Here's how it started. I fancied him, having seen him around my 'hood
a few times. We knew each other vaguely because he ran the film
programme at the place I was taking language classes – his big thing
was film. Alan ticked all the boxes: attractive, friendly, chilled out,
mysterious, with a good body but not inaccessibly hunky.

So I Facebooked him into a date. It took several attempts, but
persistence won out. At last he agreed to a drink and I had the chance
to dazzle him with smoky eyes and cleavage-happy top. I guess my
outfit worked: two drinks later he kissed me and walked me home,
and inside.

I confess that while I'd enjoyed the kiss and subsequent romping,
I wasn't set alight. Something was missing. I suppose I was just thrilled
by the triumph of getting him, and that might have clogged up my
true feelings.

So when I didn't hear from him I wasn't devastated. I could tell
what sort of thing this would be, and that was fine by me. We'd see
each other only when I put in the initiative. He was up for it, but not
enough to actually ask me out himself.

At first, I felt too lofty to be the one who got in touch after the date.
Four days later, though, I got drunk and texted him. His reply was all
smiles and 'Are you free on Friday?' As it happened, I was, and again
we had a nice drink together, enthusiastically sealed with more than
just a kiss.

Generally, because of drunken texts on my part, we kept seeing
each other once a week or so, and sometimes less – we're busy people,
evidently. Only dates one and two were drinks. Quite soon, our meetings became couply: he suggested DVDs (his taste always – arthouse
and frankly a little dull) and dinner with red wine at my place, for
example, and on weekend nights too. This was odd, because neither
the frequency of our dates nor their intensity increased. We were still

virtual strangers and made no noises about our feelings (a hallmark of the casual hook-up). I still felt a little physically numb around him, even though I was, or thought I was, attracted to him.

We didn't arrange what turned out to be our last date until the evening itself, with Alan acting true to non-committal form. He had mentioned meeting Friday night some days before, and I waited to hear what he wanted to do, assuming that even he might have the courtesy to confirm and suggest a plan a little in advance, laid-back guy though he was. Finally, at 6 p.m. that night, he deigned to get in touch, stating he'd be coming over shortly with pasta, red wine and a movie.

When he turned up, he greeted me with a languorous smooch, as though we were a couple who'd been parted for ages. In the kitchen he set about making his pasta. I stood by fixing drinks, and every now and then he'd come over to me, take me by the waist and kiss me deeply. What the hell was this? Was I his for the grasping and the smooching as we role-played our way through a domestic evening? It felt very wrong that the guy I couldn't count on even to get in touch on the day of our plan was treating me like his steady old girlfriend.

This feeling only intensified as we moved next door to the living room for the DVD. He wanted to snuggle, couple-style (he had not wanted to do this so much before), so I went along with it, my legs draped over his, his arms around me and my head resting on his shoulder. Then we retired to bed.

It was then that I knew it wasn't a goer: what happened in the bedroom made me feel about as hot as pickled herring. In the morning he wanted to stick around, but I said I really urgently had to go visit my grandparents.

What put me off was the smugness with which he seemed to think he could act like my boyfriend – all snuggles and DVDs and a morning in bed – when he'd been so unashamedly *not* my boyfriend when it came to things like reliability, communication and showing he gave even a tiny toss about seeing me. Just fifteen hours before, I was stressed because I didn't know when we'd next see each other, if at all. Now I was expected to practically bring him breakfast in bed?

What was he thinking? Were these cosy nights in just booty calls thinly disguised as romance? Or did he want me to be his Friday night sofa-mate and bed-sharer because he actually liked me? Was this just his way of showing he dug our thing because he was too arty and low-key to do it any other way?

WHAT THE GUYS THINK

ADAM L, 31, IN A COMMITTED RELATIONSHIP

Adam, our resident pick-up artist, immediately spots a guy who's just after getting laid, and who is trying to act like a player to achieve that goal. Alan is not as smooth as he thinks, but he's playing me all right.

Primary goal: getting laid

'His primary goal is getting laid. It's all about sex for this guy. If a guy's just trying to get laid, he doesn't put too much effort in. In this case he thought, "Oh, this is easy, because she's going for it. Oh, she's calling me, I'm getting laid."

'But then when he's with you it's more than that: this is the hallmark of someone trying to learn how to be a player, but who doesn't know what he's doing. He's got the "when we're together everything's going to be perfect and I'll whisk you off your feet" thing going.

'But a fully developed player would have known about putting in the extra touch. Pasta on a Friday? No way, he'd have gone further. Think of it like this: if a guy is offered a free lunch at a restaurant he's not that bothered about, he'll go for it if he doesn't have anything else too pressing to do. But if it's his favourite restaurant, he would jump at the chance to go. He'd get dressed up. He'd fit in whenever they had availability.'

But it's not just about him and his blasé attitude. He was lucky to be getting it on with me, and deep down he knew it.

'It's obvious a guy like this doesn't have a stupid amount of options,' says detective Adam. Why's that? 'You can tell a guy's prowess with women by his cooking skills: pasta is basic. If you're at pasta-level skill-base, you're way unschooled. You haven't done this much. The guy passing himself off as hard-to-pin-down hot stuff is a beginner.'

So

Sure, Alan liked me as much as the next woman, but he was motivated by two things: practising his game and getting laid. He was so pre-occupied with these, he never thought about a genuine attachment. And remember: his preoccupation bespeaks inexperience. He was acting all 'come and get it' when in fact he'd probably only slept with a small handful of women.

BRANDON L, 28, LIVES WITH HIS GIRLFRIEND

Brandon is a devil in gentleman's clothes. He's not nearly as cynical as Adam L, but he does recognize the ulterior motives of guys like Alan. He's also sympathetic to the romantic pitfalls into which men often tumble.

We know what girls are meant to like

'The truth is that most guys are not naturally empathetic in the way girls are. I've lived with my girlfriend for three years and I'm still often surprised by how bad I am at predicting her moods, at what will set her off and what won't.

'Obviously we get better over time, but especially at the beginning of the relationship we only have one thing to go on: cliché. What do I mean by this? Well, we've all seen enough *Bridget Jones*-y movies and read enough of our sisters' *Cosmos* to know what girls are meant to like: they like romantic stuff, right? And what do they think is romantic? Well, being taken out to candlelit dinners is one . . . or long languid baths where we massage them . . . or taking them to the opera . . . or booking a weekend getaway in some sexy sun-drenched place.

'These are all rather expensive or tiring. Also, in the early stages of the relationship, some of them are perhaps a little bit *too* intimate. So what can we do? Fortunately, a reliable runner-up in these romance lists is always "boyfriend cooking dinner". Perfect. It's cheap. It's comfortable. It involves alcohol. Best of all, it's a great way of seeming caring and empathetic and boyfriendy.'

The truth is all guys can cook

'The truth, though, is that all guys can cook. Especially pasta. It's the perfect boyfriendy food: it's incredibly simple to cook, but it tastes great, so impresses more than it ought. And then there's wine – usually red wine, the sexiest drink around. It's sly, it's seductive, it's an unambiguous statement that "it's on!" but in a touchy-feely new-man kind of way.

'So, there's one angle. The romantic "pasta" dinner is an incredibly easy crutch for unimaginative men to fall back on. The hope is that if we please a woman with our romantic gestures, she'll like us more and therefore be more likely to sleep with us.'

Basically, I make you pasta, you sleep with me. Brandon is coming at this from a different angle than Adam (Brandon thinks pasta is impressive), but both agree: Alan's premature boyfriendy gestures were bald attempts to achieve one thing only: getting laid.

But . . . well, it's nice to have a bit of company, right?

Out of sight, out of mind

'The truth is, these cliché romantic crutches are nice. It's nicer to watch a DVD with someone else . . . especially someone who might end up in your bed. It's comfortable and comforting to go through the dinner ritual. And the truth is guys sometimes do feel more romantic and whimsical while they're doing it . . . but then afterwards, well, that old adage "out of sight, out of mind" starts to have some effect.'

That's the killer: the guy who so romantically brought round the red wine and DVDs and hunkered down with you on the sofa before a night of sex is equally capable of forgetting you the minute he leaves – that's if he was only after one thing, of course. No wonder we get confused. I cook a romantic dinner for a man, I'm not forgetting him when I leave.

So guys find themselves torn two ways: part of them yearns for the DVD/pasta night; part of them thinks it's a total bore.

BOTTOM LINE

Sometimes these guys just need to mature, and you can certainly have fun with them while they're busy 'playing' boyfriend, all the while patting themselves on the back for being such studs. In this case, though, I'm going to take Brandon's word: 'You're well rid of him. Guys who are "into film" are best avoided. Usually the thing they lust after most is the adulation of their taste. Perhaps that's why he was so determined to force *Last Year at Marienbad* or *Hiroshima Mon Amour* or whatever down your throat that last night. If he's into pictures, then you're better off with him out of the picture.' Ha! How's that for a rule of thumb? (I personally would extend it to any guy who's self-professed 'arty'. It's great if he loves cutting-edge video installations, or deep house. But he doesn't have to inflict them on us, he really doesn't.)

What to do if you want it to develop: So, once I went off Alan, and stopped making contact with him, he started getting in touch and proposing dates. I was oddly busy. So he'd come back with more. Once I stopped being available, he couldn't get enough. I have to say I think he was also beginning to like our little meetings, and wanted more of them. He'd come round to them in his own time. So if you still fancy a guy like Alan, who seems ambivalent and blows hot and cold, you have two options. Play it so cold he thinks he might lose you, or just be chilled out while you wait for him to become attached to you. Don't give it more than four months though.

9

Why does he say he doesn't want anything, then keep ringing?

THE JIM FILES

Guys act in mystifying ways all the time. But one of the great mysteries is this one: when they claim to want nothing, but then actually seem to want something after all, just not what was originally on the table. They'll spend Friday nights watching shooting stars with you after a late one, but won't kiss you. They'll tell you they are 'confused', then hold your hand. They tell you, or make clear, that they don't want you, but then they sorta kinda do want you – in some form. What's the deal? I could never act like that towards a guy without really feeling like I'm being a shit. And if I don't want to kiss him, I sure as hell won't want to hold his hand. How can guys keep this mixed-message thing going on for so long? Doesn't it wear them down? Do they even know when they're doing it?

THE CASE

I was recently set up with Jim by someone who really should have known better: a former therapist. I should have known better too. The way she introduced him was as a successful 40-year-old just aching for a wife and kids. Now, family galore is hardly what I'm gagging for, but I was bored and frustrated by a sudden dearth of man-action, and decided to give it a go and meet him for dinner. (Only a man after a family asks you for dinner on the first blind date.)

Jim was good-looking (even with a beer belly) and I could see the potential to fancy him when I first saw him. He also worked in IT and I actually rather like a techie. But knowing he was desperate was a turn-off. As soon as we sat down I told myself this was going to be a first and last date, with him left wondering what he did wrong as I flounced back into the (single's) sunset, and me wondering what I had been thinking to meet him.

But by the end of dinner, he'd grown on me. We'd had a nice time, I was tipsy, and he hadn't seemed overeager. I wasn't sold, but I was up for more if he was. We parted with a snog but no more. A few days later he asked me out again and we had a good time. This time I invited him back to mine, and while the sex was promising at first, he didn't come for ages and after a while it kind of sucked. I was left wondering why he had struggled. Was it a lack of attraction? Bad chemistry? (See the quick-fire question on page 263.)

We hung out a few more times, and despite the annoying sex last time, I was starting to like Jim and he seemed keen. The next time we slept together, it all happened so quickly I had barely got started. This was also annoying in its own way, but a good sign nonetheless.

Jim had been pretty reliable about being in touch and things seemed to be escalating, but it was around the three-week mark I began to sense a bit of slackness. There was some vagueness about plans, fewer phone calls, and distance when we did speak. I confronted him about it sharp-ish and, lo and behold, he confessed he was feeling 'ambivalent' towards me. He'd seen a therapist that week and dug up some 'deep' stuff; the result was that I was now churning up 'uncomfortable' feelings for him. What a load of shit, I said to myself. You just don't fancy me.

Naturally this made me go from cool to obsessed. He was the one who was meant to be desperate and needy! Yet now I was desperate for another chance. Anything to bamboozle him into a few more sex sessions, so I could win him back. But all I could get out of him on the phone and over one depressing coffee was more of this 'uncomfortable feelings' bullshit and how he was feeling 'confused'.

So I left it and, predictably, didn't hear a thing for days. I forgot about Jim during the daytime, but when drunk at night I got the usual pangs and desire to text and call. Nevertheless, I managed to hold back. One night about a week after we'd last spoken, Jim rang. We had a lovely chat for forty-five minutes, but nobody mentioned 'us' or a plan to meet. It almost sounded friendly, except for the fact that it just blatantly wasn't.

Another week passed and I heard from Jim again, seemingly up for just another chat. At least this time he mentioned having got hold of a cool old French film that 'we' should watch 'sometime'.

Weird. But I couldn't help being a little encouraged, and a few nights later, while out for drinks with a friend, I sent him a little friendly text that said I was thinking of him and felt like saying hi, and that I hoped he was sheltering from the torrential rain.

He replied instantly with some cute nothing and asked how my work was going. (I'd been slaving over a big project.) I didn't reply to that, not wanting to talk work and also to see what would happen. Five minutes later he rang, and it was flirty. We talked for ten minutes before I said I had to go. Then he texted just to say how nice it had been to chat. To which I couldn't help but tell him where I was if he fancied a drink with me and my friend. He declined and, embarrassed and annoyed, I decided to leave it.

Then, after a while, he started calling me again, now with invitations. I played hard to get but he kept going, and finally we arranged to go to an exhibition together then watch a movie at his. It was a totally fun date, and he kept playing with my hands and holding them. He didn't kiss me though.

I was completely mystified. Why would he as good as tell me he's not up for it (all that therapy crap), but keep things going? Why, if I'm not the one for him, would he bother? And since he was bothering, why wasn't he keener on sex?

WHAT THE GUYS THINK

PAUL M, 31, SINGLE

Paul is not a romantic. He comes from the school of thought that believes, 'Men are primal and want to sow their seed as widely as possible.' This school basically holds that women are like new shoes that lose their shiny whiteness after a few shags – or even just one. Ick.

Less arousing

'It is quite common for men to lose interest in a woman they aren't obsessively desirous of after sex. This is defined as PEGOOMHS (Post-Ejaculatory Get-Out-of-My-House Syndrome). Regular sex with the most attractive woman in the world will, eventually, become less arousing and less interesting. I have lost count of the number of times my male friends, all with attractive girlfriends, have said to me that sex has become an obligation rather than something they look forward to.'

Something else

'I think this is because what drives sexual desire in men is wanting what they can't have. Once a man has a girlfriend there is no challenge, no thrill of the chase. Once he has a girlfriend the idea of sleeping with other women arouses him, because he can't, or shouldn't, have them. So in order for a man to want to continue in a relationship and not ditch every girl he sleeps with after the first few couplings, he has to think there is something else he wants that he doesn't yet have. He then decides whether the woman is the kind who can mother their kids or, more importantly, mother him.'

So

Jim got bored. His own sex performance aside, as far as he was concerned, he'd bedded me and I'd given in too easily. I'd left him with nothing else to want or go after. Since I lacked what he saw as mother-of-his-child (or even just girlfriend) qualities, he went off me, hence the non-committal texting.

NICK L, 29, MARRIED

Nick is a die-hard rationalist – with computers (he's a software engineer), with maths and with women. He takes the view that we make things a lot more complicated than they are.

True man style

'Men tend to behave fairly directly, and they assume that everyone behaves the same way. Ergo, the best way to work out what Jim is thinking is simply to study his behaviour and take it at face value. When he first meets you, he seems quite keen. He's probably been single for a while, and you're attractive, so naturally enough he's flirty and keen to pursue some kind of relationship.

'After a while he starts to cool towards you. It may be that he's met another girl that he likes better, or it may simply be that after the initial thrill of dating, he's realized that you don't have much in common, or that you're not as pretty as he thought, or even that your personality isn't his cup of tea.'

Whatever it is, when a guy acts cool, he feels cool. Do not do what I always do: try to explain his behaviour with all the reasons in the world except his feelings towards you. He's gone off you.

'Perhaps he gets the impression that you're judging him on his sexual performance. Not everyone likes that.'

Never mind the fact that he performed badly – how are we to blame? Women give the benefit of the doubt to a fault, I find.

'Anyway, in true man style he comes right out and tells you that he's feeling ambivalent towards you. That word "ambivalent" isn't code for anything; it's not a cryptic clue that needs to be deciphered. The great thing about men is that they mostly lack any kind of guile when it comes to relationship politics; they simply come right out and say what they're feeling.'

A controversial, but oddly compelling argument.

Friendship

'Later, Jim feels like calling you. It is fairly clear from the call that Jim is not calling to get back with you. If he was, he'd say, "Let's get back together." If he was shy or embarrassed he might arrange to meet up first. He doesn't do either of these things. He is friendly. This is because he wants to be friends.'

But doesn't he have enough friends? Why would he want to be just friends with someone with whom the established bond is sexual and it's only going to get messy?

'There are a few reasons. He may be feeling guilty about dumping you; he may be doubting his decision (absence makes the heart grow fonder and all that); he may be following some kind of misplaced ideal that now you've had time to cool off he should make an effort to be friends with you so you don't end up as another "crazy ex" that he has to cross the street to avoid.'

Men enjoy flirting, like anyone

'You then send Jim a flirty text. Because flirting is enjoyable in and of itself, men and women will often flirt with people that they don't intend to start up a relationship with, especially when drunk.

'Jim is behaving like a man who doesn't really fancy you but likes you enough to want to occasionally chat or spend time together as friends, and sometimes can't help skirting the friendly/flirty border because of your past history.'

So

Jim, like many men, is simply talking and acting in accordance with his feelings and thoughts. He was lukewarm because he had doubts. What I took as stringing along was behaviour caused by these factors: a) flirting is fun in and of itself; and b) he was interested in friendship – for several possible reasons, one of them being guilt. (But guys do admit they string girls along. See the quick-fire question on page 143 for when, how and why. And they're not straight talkers all the time either: see the quick-fire question on page 38 about the biggest excuses men give when they're not keen. Rarely is that excuse 'I'm not keen'.)

BOTTOM LINE

He went off me. He decided I wasn't wife material enough to merit the effort (and boredom?) of easy old sex. Whatever it was that put him off pursuing a relationship with me, when he said he felt 'ambivalent' towards me, he meant it.

The continuous contact was explained by non-romantic things: keeping his options open, desiring friendship and following up on some second thoughts. One thing is clear, Jim was not suddenly going to give me something serious, and I should have been explicit about what I wanted instead of playing games. As I wasn't that into him, I should have stopped answering his calls. If I did want something, I needed to tell him so, then walk away if and when he didn't come through. Most of all, I wish I'd controlled my high hopes and stopped trying to work out what his 'ambivalent' gestures *meant*. Because in the vast majority of cases, the proof is in the pudding. And the pudding was undercooked and a bit tasteless here.

What to do if you fancy a Jim: I really want to tell you to gather your dignity, because in playing along with his little game, you're getting your hopes up and wasting your energy. You'll take hit after hit of disappointment and confusion, while he stays in control. Lame, especially when your greatness could and should be getting some love elsewhere.

On the other hand, it's unbelievably hard to walk away and break off contact when a guy you fancy keeps getting in touch, giving mixed signals. I'd say: come clean. If you want a relationship, tell him, in clear terms. If he is forced to clarify that he won't give you that, you'll find it easier to get over him. And perhaps the ultimatum 'Give me a relationship or I'm out of here' will jolt him into action. Nothing is sexier in a woman than the resolve to walk away.

NB: as a rule of thumb, when you think you are receiving mixed signals, they're not usually very mixed. It's more likely that a guy is taking his time to enjoy your interest before he fades away entirely from your life. Cynical but, in cases like Jim's, true.

10

Why does he bother with grand gestures, then fail to follow through?

THE FRANK FILES

Every girl, no matter how independent and cynical, wants to be swept off her feet. Dear God, I'm putty in the hands of a man who buys me flowers or champagne. Could there be a sadder, more clichéd confession from someone who thinks of herself as a feminist?

But even the most sensible of us have a huge capacity for grand romantic gestures, because they make us feel loved, and we all want to – and think we should – be loved. C'mon, we do. My friend Jo encapsulates it in a simple phrase: she'll caution me not to be too 'love me' on the phone to a guy. She believes all women are not far off wearing signs that scream these two words in various shades of hot pink. I kind of have to agree.

So, this whole grand-gesture-equals-love equation is hard to shake, even though we should know better. I mean, in the old days, chivalry and shameless wooing were de rigueur even if you weren't going to get into somebody's pants, ever. Now we're in a post-romantic age and it's all about subtle or no gestures, big gloopy ones carry a major, dangerously effective wow factor. (Nothing cheesy or creepy, mind. It can be a thin line.)

It's all very well for a guy to do the big gestures when the time is right. But what I've never understood is why he does them when he's about to bugger off. I'm not talking about obvious arseholery here, or pick-up artistry for its own sake. I'm talking about similar situations to the one my friend Marissa found herself in last year – when the guy really seems to mean it, wants to mean it, has no cause not to mean it since he's the initiator, then buggers off all the same.

THE CASE

My friend Marissa (29 and blessed with a mane of voluminous blonde hair) was at her parents' thirtieth wedding anniversary in Edinburgh. She was just minding her own business and having a dance with mates when suddenly Frank – an older man with gorgeous, slightly creased green eyes – appeared. She wasn't too bothered, being used to come-ons from all manner of eligible men, but he had maturity on his side, and for a woman like Marissa who'd had it with disappointing twenty-somethings this gave him an in.

He'd spied her across the room (it's hard to resist that hair, and Marissa always looks like she's having the best time), and set his sights on her. She didn't play very hard to get – she's not into games – and went along with him to his hotel room. Hell, she's up for as much fun as the next girl and felt like a little post-party naughty business. Nothing else.

So when she left the next morning amid his promises to call her, she was as cool as a cucumber (well, maybe a little ruffled), and not overly bothered. She'd barely had time to get back to London when a handwritten note was pushed through the letter-box inviting her to dinner the next night. He wined and dined her and they had a lovely time, though she was still on her guard: guys like this are usually up to something.

Two days later, when a first-class return ticket to Moscow (yes, Moscow, and yes, first class) came through her letter-box – he was going there on business the next day – she gulped and went along with it. Who wouldn't? He met her at the airport with flowers and designer vodka and ferried her off to his hotel suite. They spent a magical few days together (how couldn't they?), and she was just starting to come round to the idea that all these gestures were an artless function of his deep and solid passion for her.

Of course, part of her remained a little wary still, 'too good to be true' pounding in her temples. When he'd left her at the airport, he'd talked like he meant to go on in this vein, finding a way in his busy international schedule to make time for her, and so on.

When she'd heard nothing the next day, she sniffed trouble. When the silence continued for three more days, she knew it was only a matter of time before she found out that Frank was indeed too good to be true. The email (!) arrived one week after she returned from Moscow. Frank said work had been crazy and that while he thought Marissa was a nice girl he couldn't see it working through this period of intense travel and research for his next project. Marissa laughed a little, felt a bit bummed out because she'd fallen for his tricks, but was glad he hadn't dragged it out any further.

But what had he been playing at? He could have made the same grand gestures while making it clear it was all whim, a spur-of-the-moment thing. Instead, he went on about how amazing she was and how he could see them together. The combination of dinners, a flight and chats about the long term sure made his sudden frost odd. Was he a pathological romantic? An evil manipulating player? Or had he just gone off her?

WHAT THE GUYS THINK

PETER W, 51, MARRIED TWICE

Peter is the oldest panel member here. But far from reminding me of my dad, he's even worse than a young man, at least in identifying (and, I bet, identifying with) the male motive for feverish pursuit followed by sudden rejection. Let's just say it has to do with a word that begins with *f* and ends with *g*. Note the sports imagery too: you'd never guess he was American, would you?

Mr Virility

'Obviously this guy is a professional bachelor. Intensely driven to get the girl into bed. That achieved – goal scored! – he got bored with her and hankered for the next one.'

Simple as that! How shallow can you be? Then again, as Victor (my ex-flatmate's boyfriend) put it, men are built to 'sow their seed', whereas women who shag competitively are motivated by more complex, less biological factors. I think he's right. That said, I won't accept the idea that men can get away with shitty behaviour because they're 'built' for it. Just to be clear.

'He hankered for the next . . . and the next,' continues Peter. 'He's rich, attractive, permanently single and loves to fuck new girls. Mr Virility. The more the better. But it's the newness that is attractive (not the chase, as some would have you believe). Another conquest! Another one to add to the "feel pretty darn good about myself" list. Now it's time to cut loose and check out the new girl over there.'

So

New, new, new. Score that goal. Wham bam, I'm a man. He's driven by bed-notches and novelty only. Could it be? Even with a man as seemingly civilized as Frank? With a guy who knows what designer vodka is? Apparently so.

VICTOR L, 28, IN A SERIOUS RELATIONSHIP

Reading back over his own words here, Victor roared with satisfaction. 'This is just so true,' he said. 'It is just so, so true.' He's a bit of a traditionalist is Victor, and he exaggerates the needs of the male ego. Still, I think you'll find he knows his stuff. I for one found his words super-helpful.

Want her thinking about how great he is

'There's no question that a guy wants to sweep a girl off her feet as quickly as possible. This is fact. Guys just do that, they want her thinking about him and how great he is. The quicker she falls for him, the more secure the guy will feel, and he'll be able to sit back, sigh and assess this "new girl". Once in this comfort zone, he will think about whether he truly wants her now the chase was successful.

'He may have in fact decided way earlier on that she wasn't for him, but he got too caught up in everything for different reasons, such as trying to get over someone, the sex, or general boredom, which is very cruel. Once he saw it was getting serious (which was his doing in the first place), he ran.'

Flat-out initially

'Many guys do go flat-out with a girl initially, then leave it suddenly. One of my best friends seems to do this, finding out only after wooing her senseless that he is now bored. I think this is because he is insecure, he loves being loved and wants her to fall for him as quickly as possible. A girl who shows initial interest but doesn't fall for him leaves a serious bruise on a man's ego.

'Once fallen, this man can now decide what to do, knowing his ego is fine whatever the decision.'

So

Frank needs to be loved – repeatedly – but he does not need to love, and once Marissa showed signs of falling for him, he got bored.

BOTTOM LINE

This sort of man is on a permanent, ego-aggrandizing roll, and you'll just get rolled over unless you step out of the way. Marissa's only hope was to keep her distance – perhaps for ever. Worth it if you like the high life and have enough inner confidence and self-esteem to play it cooler than most of us are capable of doing.

What to do if you still fancy him: Be disciplined about holding back. Do not agree to every arrangement, every dinner date, so quickly; do not go along with every woo. This might well give him enough space to figure out that he wants you, rather than giving him the instant gratification he is seeking from you. (But don't hold your breath.) Steel yourself against the attractions of his money and glamour. And ask yourself very loudly and clearly if the extravagant romantic gestures in the short term are worth it for the medium-term cooling off that is the trademark of this particular type of man. It may not be a problem for you: if, for example, you're on the rebound, it could be just the thing you need. Or perhaps you're such a storyteller that you'd see him just to talk about it over cocktails with your girlfriends (that would be me). But if you have a history of getting hooked and not taking coldness or playing games well, try, try, try to avoid this guy.

11

Why won't he end it when he's clearly miserable?

THE MARK FILES

Nothing breaks my heart more than seeing a friend trying to please her grumpy, distant man, and making excuses for why she hasn't seen him in days and why he was horrible to her that night you were all out together. Finally the guy makes her so miserable, acts so plainly like a cock to her, that she has to end it. Know that pattern? I've seen it loads of times.

But I've never understood why guys so often let things sour for ages, effectively forcing the girl to end it. And I'll be honest: sometimes I don't even understand why something sours *at all* when it had seemed so perfect. Why do men go off us one fine day, but then hang about being mean and horrid as the love ebbs slowly and painfully away? Remember the Steve Files in Chapter 3? It was agony to watch Steve going chilly – and then nasty – after being with Alice for a year.

THE CASE

Vicky was actually on a mission to set Mark up with her friend Anna when they accidentally hooked up instead at a gig in their hometown of Birmingham last year. Vicky had come wearing stilettos and a miniskirt, got drunk, and what with all the toing and froing between Mark and Anna, actually ended up falling into bed with him herself.

A weekend together followed, with baths and DVDs and all-round 'wow, we are really hitting it off' amazement going on.

They were one of those cool couples that just seemed to get on with it without a fanfare; before we knew it, Vicky's answer to the question of what she was doing that night was, 'Mark's coming over.' She fell for him, hard.

But after four months or so, Mark began to seem preoccupied: less keen on spending time at Vicky's, and more intent on doing his own thing. He began to make her feel bad, and she started trying to figure out what was wrong and get around it. As so often happens, it looked like a case of commitment phobia. In response, Vicky tried to tone down anything that could resemble neediness. She began second-guessing everything and making excuses for his behaviour: maybe Mark wasn't up for a relationship because of this or that reason; maybe she was too demanding and expected too much. They certainly didn't appear to be in a relationship, more in some unpleasant limbo.

The obvious reality was that he'd lost interest, or, for whatever reason, just wasn't playing ball. We all waited for him to end it, as she was too in love with him to do it. He grew more and more tetchy around Vicky; it was almost as though she annoyed him.

And yet the months stretched on with some semblance of a relationship. A few times a week, Vicky would receive him in whatever mood in which he cared to turn up, and she'd say they were still 'together'. Usually, his mood was bad or inaccessible.

*

Finally, eight months after they met, things came to a head. His lack of interest and all the other fallings-off of the last few months came to breaking point, and even the in-love Vicky had to let things go. They had a talk – initiated by her – and broke up.

Now, it's well known that men will go out of their way to avoid drama and waterworks, even if that means not breaking up with someone they don't want to be with. But four months? What on earth kept Mark in the limbo situation with Vicky for such a long time? He radiated the vibes of a man who didn't want to continue things, so why did he? It couldn't have been simply because of the sex and the fear of drama. Mark is universally regarded as a hot guy: finding women to sleep with wouldn't have been an issue. More to the point, he's a relationship guy and has based his sexual life within that context; it also means he knows how to end things with women. Did he drag it out just for inertia's sake? Or for the sex?

WHAT THE GUYS THINK

MAOR E, 30, IN A RELATIONSHIP

Serial monogamist Maor's big thing is that our grief is our own fault, i.e. we don't walk away from guys when they don't give us what we want, so we can hardly be surprised if we're miserable. He is adamant that we should ask for what we want and deserve, and if we don't get it, leave. (Go figure: he's been on the receiving end of miserable women waiting for him to deliver something he's not going to.) Easier said than done, obviously. On the other hand, it's not impossible. But first, a reminder that guys don't necessarily become attached like we do.

Not his girlfriend

'She called him her boyfriend, but I reckon he didn't describe her in his head as his girlfriend. So basically she was in a limbo situation.

There's a category for guys where we can see a woman as more than a fuck-buddy but less than a girlfriend.'

Women just do not have that category. Hence the confusion. God, men can be cold-hearted.

'As a man you can be in a phase where you like being with someone because you like sleeping with her and it's available and she's not giving you a hard time about it. It's easy. And guys can keep going like that – sex with someone nice, hot and undemanding – indefinitely.'

And why not? But for all but the most Samantha Jones-esque women, this pleasant, easy-sex relationship is a one-way street of satisfaction. That is, for the guy.

'If Vicky knew that she really cared about Mark and wanted more from him, she should have demanded it. If that didn't work, there was no future for them as boyfriend and girlfriend.'

Not his fault

'She should have given him the ultimatum. That's the thing with women sometimes, they just don't have the courage to end it. It's not the guy's fault, it's the woman's; after four months you should know how it's going and if you like it. Women should take more responsibility: if she wants something and she's not getting it, she should talk to him about it. Chances are, though, if he's into her they won't get to that place.'

Women should take more responsibility. Hardly the response you'd expect when the guy is the one acting like a tosser. But though it doesn't sound like it, this is actually a woman-friendly comment. We need to get tough and have the courage to walk away. If we hang about for sub-standard treatment, it's our fault when we get it. Thing is, I don't know about you, but part of me fears walking away in case I can't find anyone else. Awful, but true. Anyway, now we come to the dilemma of whether or not to throw away the cake when you're both having and eating it.

'Maybe he just couldn't handle blowing her off: on one hand he's getting the attention, but on the other hand he's not sure he wants it, it's just he's got nothing else going on. It's not true that if a man is good-looking he can get sex easily – even Mark might have felt he needed to stay with Vicky just for sex. And once you've got something with someone that already exists, it's not easy to give it up.

'He acted like a man; don't blame him. The woman should be able to demand what she needs and wants and, if she's not getting what she deserves, to walk out of it, and that's it.'

So

Mark had a good reason to drag things out: sex with someone he probably quite liked and who didn't give him a hard time. But he didn't see her as his girlfriend; if he had done, things wouldn't have got to where they were. In such cases, the girl should lay out her feelings and expectations, and if they aren't met, walk away. Since she didn't challenge him, it's her fault they continued unsatisfactorily. The moral of the story is actually huge: women, remember you're great, and you deserve what you want. Don't just reduce your needs and expectations to fit the agenda of a guy who is making you feel lonely, despairing and rubbish.

JEREMY A, 40, ENGAGED

Jeremy is a wise man who has run the gamut of relationships. Although he appears to opt for the 'men are wimps or bastards' line of thought, it is not quite as simple as that.

Didn't have the balls

'I really wanted to stick up for the bloke here, but I can't. I would like to think that he was comfortable with the situation – she's good company, great arm candy and a hot shag, and at his stage in life he doesn't really want anything else. But the moodiness and unreliability suggests that he really wanted out, but didn't have the balls to call it a day.'

Right thing, wrong reasons

'This is not all bad. I've done this, as have many blokes. And I did it because I didn't want to upset someone who I had shared some good times with and cared about. I was young. I was wrong. But I felt I was doing the right thing at the time. In other words, Mark was wrong but for the right reasons.

'Quite why she kept it going for so long is the real mystery here. It sounds like he was doing all he could to finish things (apart from, erm, finishing them) and she, in some Jane Austen-like romantic haze, wanted to keep things going. Most men don't do "feelings". They don't have those "we need to talk" conversations. That's up to the girls.'

Up to us. Just like walking away when we're not happy. Looks like if you want to know a guy's intentions, you have to pay attention to his actions, not his words. It's the same as when you get together: he'll *show* you how keen he is, he won't tell you. Also, 'Jane Austen-like haze'? Evidently some men really think of period dramas and frilly dresses and hysteria when it comes to our wanting to be with them.

So

Mark made the schoolboy error of trying to avoid hurting Vicky by not spelling out what he was thinking, wanting or feeling. But that's hardly a surprise seeing as 'most men don't do "feelings".' Again, it was Vicky's job to take the hint and pull the plug. But Mark was a bit of a cock for allowing his fear of actually breaking up with Vicky to stop him doing so. Instead he just let her suffer.

BOTTOM LINE

Mark was getting what he wanted here, at least for a while, and could get away with having sex on his own terms without the commitment. Then, he wanted out, but couldn't quite bring himself to finish it, for fear of hurting Vicky (maybe) and also out of genuine puzzlement about whether it was worth giving up the sex.

What to do if you're stuck with a Mark: Remember that you are great. Remember you have courage and self-respect and that life is too short. Rally it all and demand what you want. Once you've reached the four-month mark you need to come clean about the degree of your feelings. Don't sell yourself short. Had Vicky laid out her demands and, not having had them met, walked away, it's quite likely Mark would have come running back. He might have realized he missed her, and he'd respect her more. But don't do it as a tactic, because he might well not miss you. Basically, don't do it for him. Do it for number one.

Quick-fire questions 3

How do you know it's serious?

GREG D: 'I'll wait a little longer to make a plan with the guys: I'll keep big nights like Thursday or Saturday free for the girl. I'd normally not have dates at the weekend because those are priority days – you know when you start doing those things it's getting serious. The other thing is after-sex activity: right after sex, libido is actually at a negative level, so if you're still cuddling or flirting that's a good sign; it means there's nothing but raw feelings. These are the only five minutes in life when there's no libido at all for a guy.'

ALECK F: 'To me I know if it's serious from the start: the kinds of conversation that you have at three in the morning. Basically, I think you reveal more embarrassing shit if you're hitting it off with her and feel comfortable and are into her. As a rule I've found that it's only in short-term relationships that I know are going to be short-term from the start that I think about things like how often to call, or whatever.'

JOE P: 'The usuals, I'm afraid: I would never introduce a girl to my family unless I thought we were going to be very serious.'

Why is breaking up with a girl so scary?

DAVID A: 'The thought of what comes after a break-up, when you have to consider the prospect of a lifetime of singledom. But I'm one of those pig-headed men who would either be callous about splitting up, because I didn't love the girl, and I thought we would both be better off apart, and therefore would expect her to cope as well as I would, or self-pitying, because I would convince myself that it is my lot in life to be alone. This last reaction is rather childish and unattractive, which fuels the self-pity. Being scared doesn't really come into it.'

ROBIN H: 'The possibility that her reaction will expose me as a complete bastard. I think it's relatively easy to convince yourself that dumping someone is the right thing for everyone, that they won't be that hurt, and that you have in fact been honest, reasonable, considerate, etc. in your actions to date. The scary thing is that when you follow through on that line of reasoning and make real the step that seems so well considered in your mind, it gets a lot more messy and the arguments that sounded so convincing no longer make any sense. There may indeed be an accusation that such flimsy justifications as I have attempted to provide are themselves self-serving, dishonest or cowardly, and worst of all there is every chance that I will end up agreeing with my accuser that actually all the things I have been telling myself are nonsense I made up to make myself feel better about being heartless and deceptive.'

Do you ever agonize over sending texts/calling?

MARK C: 'Only really when I'm still getting to know someone, in which case I endlessly redraft texts to make sure they are perfect and then I anxiously wait for their reply. Years ago, when calling girls, I used to walk about a mile and a half to the nearest phone box to make the call because I was too nervous to phone from my own house. What that says about me I don't know and I'm happy to say I grew out of that habit years ago.'

RON E: 'Yes, I do. Women as we all know respond much better to the written word and texting is an incredibly important art to master. Bear in mind that I only go out with girls with liberal arts degrees (not as a rule, but it's turned out that way). Send good texts and you are in there. And it's so easy! Women pay attention to words, little things, nuances, and so it's reasonable to give their missives careful attention.'

Do you wait a few hours before answering a text – i.e. do you play the game?

KOBI N: 'With someone I'm not into, I would put off writing back. In other cases I play a more sophisticated game, as in bringing up other girls or so on.'

NICK H: 'Depends on the circumstances. I don't like the

game, but sometimes it's a necessity, just as a way of
protecting ourselves.'

**Do you find it hard to be alone – i.e. do you always fill the
gaps, even when you're not that into someone?**

KARL C: 'I always try to fill in the gaps; it gets me down to
be on a dry spell. I always make sure there is a partner
for sex.'

TOM A: 'It's a question of maturity. Let's face it. When guys
are young and spotty, they're thrilled if anybody's interested. At that stage we will fill the gap and go out with
anybody. Anybody at all, in fact. This changes. Very slowly
– never underestimate male insecurity. Eventually, though,
we realize that girls are actually attracted to us. It's not
just some mistake. There'll be more comers. Then we can
start being picky. Nowadays, I ask myself: do I really want
to bear this girl with her horrible voice? She has great tits.
But she's also been droning on about how badly everyone
treats her for the last hour. And because I now know I can
do better, off I go.'

**What goes through your mind when a girl offers to go halves
on the bill? Do you think she's polite or not interested?**

GAVIN R: 'I'd appreciate the gesture but would softly insist
on paying. (If she genuinely wants to and I thought I'd
offend if I didn't let her, then I would let her.) I'd genuinely think it was nice (not that I'd dislike it the other
way) because I'd want to end up in a relationship that is
morally fifty-fifity (i.e. give and take, both contribute in
some way, with financial contributions along Marxist

lines). I wouldn't want to end up in a situation where I was just a cash cow and so these token gestures can be important. But the first date is a bit early for that. I'd see it as a small net positive (unless it felt fake) but would not really be fussed either way.'

KEVIN B: 'If she offers, the alpha male in me definitely kicks in. I always try to pay, although it is polite for a girl to offer. I think it shows that you are equals.'

RICHARD L: 'For me, her offering doesn't give me the impression she's not interested. Nowadays it seems to be a polite phrase they like to use to make us aware that we should be paying for the meal. I'm happy to pay the whole thing without question, but I guess it's always nice to hear the offer. Although if she's minted then I have no problem having the cheque picked up for me.'

PART FOUR
Physical Dead End

When you think something's going to happen – even just a snog – it absolutely sucks when it doesn't. In fact, it's a pet issue of mine. That's because it seems like you're being physically rejected. Which is the fastest way for you to feel like it's because you're ugly/fat/spotty. And that can make you cry and curse the world.

As for why it's a pet issue, well, it's happened to me a lot. There were whole years of my adolescence where I was led to think, and hoped against hope, that so and so would kiss me, and sometimes it seemed just about to happen . . . and it didn't. I became sensitive to it, as though I was physically unappealing in some fundamental way (I wasn't) or rather, that something about me just screamed 'friend' while something about my friends screamed 'kiss/fancy me'. I felt doomed.

Naturally, things changed after a while. But every now and then – between the flings and snogs and so forth – my post-adolescence has been punctuated with a few too many (for my liking) episodes of physical let-downs.

I guess I've always had the idea that men are supposed to be horny and up for it, and when they're not, something is seriously wrong. Writing this book has taught me this is not the case. Chapter 14, about Lasse, is the ultimate example. I was wondering why he was turning down a second night of sex in a row. It transpires that no guy in his right mind wants sex again the very next night if they are having a fling. Read on to find out why. And in the Quick-fire section, guys reveal that it's OK (and normal) for a guy not to always be up for sex with his girlfriend.

But of course, physical dead ends aren't just about a simple

absence of action. In fact, they're most pronounced *after* some physical action. That is, a hook-up usually engenders another hook-up, or
at least the expectation of one (assuming normal circumstances
where there's nothing to lose, the hook-up was pleasant and the guy
seemed keen). When it fails to work that way, it can be deeply troub-
ling. Why did he go off me? The most painful example of this is the
old-friend-to-lover move, where it seems initially like a match made
in heaven because best friends enter lover status at a deeper level.
Yet while the chemistry can be overwhelming when two friends are
still technically just friends, once they get together it is often the case
that the guy stops fancying the girl. Find out why by reading the
Charlie Files in Chapter 15.

The other two chapters in this section are about Raphael and Aaron.
Raphael left me feeling really confused and shitty (for a night), whereas
Aaron just left me scratching my head. There are reasons why a guy
won't kiss you. But it's unlikely to be that you're ugly . . . which is
something to be grateful for. Still, just to be sure, I asked guys this:
'Has it ever happened that a girl seemed attractive to you until you
saw her naked?' (see page 148). There's a bunch of other questions
and answers that might also help to explain those mysterious moments
when a guy is anything but all over you.

12

Why does he flirt and invite you over, without making a move?

THE RAPHAEL FILES

Guys are, in general, horny, sex-crazed and always up for it. At any rate, that's the going idea. Of course, not every guy is like that. And anyone who has had a relationship will tell you that even the horniest guy sometimes can't be bothered. But basically, guys want sex. Any number of blokes will confirm that. My friend Johnnie always talks about 'gender programming' and 'seed-sowing'. Horrific terms, I know, but hey. As a woman, I'm partial to a bit of that seed-sowing spirit (minus the sowing).

So it's always flustering when, as happens every so often in life, you meet men who seem utterly unmoved by the prospect of sex. These guys aren't just tired, or burnt out, or drunk, they're uninterested, and probably afraid of it too. It makes a change from the usual complaints about blokes being motivated only by sex, but not, in my book, a pleasant change.

I'm not talking about when they're not up for it because they don't fancy you. What troubles and mystifies me is when they seem to want you – they pick you out, chat you up, woo you, go through the gestures of someone who wants some action – and then they slither away from it, leaving you standing there with your mouth open, tongue hanging out and wondering if it's because you're ugly. What is going on with these guys? Is it me or them?

THE CASE

Raphael, a French music promoter, got in touch on Facebook, claiming to think I was another Zoe he knew. Usually I don't respond to blind internet approaches, but I had a good look at his profile and he was just about the hottest guy I'd ever seen. I checked that his profile pic wasn't actually of a famous person, and it looked real.

The banter was deeply flirtatious, a tone entirely set by him. Before I knew it, he proposed drinks (on him, of course). I knew that even if I looked my best, I was still an ordinary mortal and not some god as he so clearly was.

He tipped up, fresh from the gym, his tan, muscular torso practically still quivering from the exertion. My tongue almost fell out, but then I pulled myself together. I'm always on my guard with guys this good-looking and I wasn't about to start feeling inferior just because he was hot. He'd better be interesting too.

So I relaxed and was myself, since I'd decided I should be seeing what he had to offer me, him having been the keen bean. All the same, I held back. Gods don't mix with mortals and I wasn't about to make a fool of myself. He kept buying me drinks, getting me drunker. I still couldn't tell what his intentions or feelings were, but when we got outside to catch the bus, he kissed me – not the other way round.

I was thrilled that such a hottie had swooped in, but wasn't about to hold my breath since we were both pretty pissed. All the same, as soon as we got on the 82 bus he asked me what I was doing that weekend. I said I was free on Friday and, with romantic urgency, the French accent extra strong, he said, 'Fine, I see you Friday.'

The next day he texted – with two kisses at the end – to say he'd jumped the gun and that he had other plans that Friday but would love to reschedule. Bad he cancelled; good he seemed energetically up for rescheduling.

We kept texting – often several times a day, very flirty. Eventually (maybe two or three weeks later) we arranged to meet. He took me out for dinner, quizzed me about my relationship history and kept saying he could tell I was super-intelligent, smarter than him. Again, his intentions were unclear: on the one hand his questions, flirtatious-ness and insistence on paying for dinner and drinks implied he fancied me; on the other, the fact that I was unsure meant something was off.

After one post-dinner drink he claimed exhaustion. He hailed me a cab but didn't get in, and only kissed me for a millisecond on the lips, apologizing and again pleading tiredness. As we all know, tiredness never stopped a man who wants to give you a massive snog and go home with you, so I took the hint and tried to forget about it.

Which would have been possible if he hadn't kept being in touch. But always there with the texts and the flirtation he was. Why bother?

Anyway, one Saturday night I was out with friends when we began having a text interchange. The result was that he invited me round to his flat for karaoke. I got there at about 12.30. His flatmate was there with his girlfriend, and it sure looked like I was the girlfriend-figure for Raphael – it was just the four of us. But the karaoke went on and on, and I got more and more annoyed. Yet I was curious: was this seriously all friend stuff? Had he really invited me to his flat late on a Saturday night to be his singing companion? Finally, the flat was invaded by his other flatmates and the possibility of a 'moment' between us vanished. Just as I was about to leave, Raphael invited me up to his room. I knew for sure this was going to lead to something: 27-year-old men do not invite girls to their bedrooms to chat.

Or so I thought. We got up there, and, like a hyperactive child, he grabbed his guitar and started strumming. I sat by, waiting for him to make a move, not believing I had stayed up until 3 a.m. for this. But he kept going with the concert, until it suddenly dawned on me that I could stay till sunrise and nothing would happen. I forced myself to call a cab, loathe to leave without any sequel whatsoever to our first snogging session but acutely aware he'd probably hoped I'd leave ages ago.

After this, we stopped communicating; he knew he'd blown it as well as I. What had happened though to explain our month or more of relentless flirting, that one snog and a host of empty signs? It was a waste of my time once I saw that nothing was happening; had he known all along he wasn't up for anything? If that was the case, why did he deliberately try to waste his own time?

WHAT THE GUYS THINK

JAMES M, 24, IN A RELATIONSHIP

James is the sweetest guy on earth, and goes out with a good friend of mine. He pursued her like crazy – like a tiger on the prowl, even though he's so soft-spoken and gentle. Anyway, the point is, he knows something about going after intelligent women, and about pursuit in general. He seemed just the man to ask about Raphael.

Intellect is an obstacle

'It's interesting that Raphael liked your intelligence. This instantly makes me think of the old chestnut that men are often more attracted to women with whom they can feel intellectually superior and empowered by their sense of being the "man", or the breadwinner. And from what I've read, this is particularly pertinent to high-earners like bankers. Perhaps your intellect, though clearly of interest to him, so much interest that he kept asking you out on dates, was an obstacle to him taking the relationship to other levels.'

Intelligence again. That famous turn-off. Ladies, beware guys who seem to have it all. They're not going to feel at ease with someone who seems to have even more, particularly in the way of brains. But can you imagine a smart woman preferring a sillier man? God, no.

'The whole "concert" incident suggests Raphael is a poser and enjoys attention. It's possible that he continued texting and flirting with you because he was enjoying it, but I reckon he just liked the attention, and that's all he wanted.'

When you look too admiringly on a guy (I was probably watching the guitar-playing as though it was the resurrection of Jimi Hendrix), you could be giving him the only reason to keep it going. Which back-fires on you, because you're only doing it so that he will adore you.

Lack of physical attraction

'Basically, the attention of an intelligent girl is no substitute for roman-tic interest. He just wasn't interested in you romantically. The first time he kissed you, which is the only real indication that there was ever any interest on Raphael's part, happened after a lot of drinking and at the end of a fun evening. I'd say he was genuinely enjoying your company but that there wasn't enough of a physical attraction for him to want to take it further.'

So

He was into the attention resulting from his texts, and he enjoyed – but was also turned off by – my intelligence. There was no romantic intent on his part, just a motivation for pleasurable attention-grabbing and flirting. The kiss was just a circumstantial thing. It signified nothing but excitement at the end of a fun night. Lesson: don't read meaning into physical actions. Guys will kiss you, even shag you, based on a that-moment-only whim.

NADAV H, 28, MAN ABOUT TOWN

Let's just say that Nadav is a bit of a Romeo in his hometown of Tel
Aviv. On one hand, he's a total stud; on the other, you'd never imagine
it. He's soft-spoken, almost effeminate. And very sensitive. He explains
why sometimes he doesn't make a move.

Just can't touch

'It is possible that he has some issue with sex, but I don't think that's
the case. Take me, for example. I don't think I have any weird issue
with it and usually I enjoy it very much. But until some time ago, I
could never ever make the first move. Not even when I sat in my
bedroom with a beautiful girl at 3 a.m. I would probably feel more
comfortable picking up the guitar. It's a self-confidence thing – or a
lack thereof. I clearly remember girls who felt the same way with me
as you do here, when I gave them the 3 a.m. concert. Even so, all I
could do was go on playing. Sometimes you just can't touch a girl even
if you really want to. It's like you're frozen by an irrational fear of being
rejected, even though you know you won't be.'

So

Well, that's reassuring. Sometimes guys can't make the first move,
exactly like us. Only they know they're the ones who are supposed to,
so the pressure sometimes drives them to do things like playing the
guitar as an alternative way of gaining approval. Or killing time.

But a word of warning with this excuse: nine times out of ten the guy
doesn't make the first move because he's not into it. Sure, there are
exceptions, like Nadav. You have to gauge the situation and the kind of
guy. I have to say, for all his good looks, Raphael did seem insecure and
nervy. If I'd jumped him he'd probably have gone with it. But I don't
think we'd have had much of a future – even a fling-term one. So it would
have only heaped confusion on things because I'd have been sitting there
expecting something – even something small – if we'd romped around.

BOTTOM LINE

There may be an irrational fear factor going on, no matter how good-looking he is. But the chances are the physical connection just isn't powerful enough, otherwise – in this case – Raphael would have made it clearer what he wanted. Still, just in case it is a problem with nerves or being frozen by fear of rejection, I'd say you might as well make the move and see what happens. The worst that can happen is embarrassment.

What to do if you're unsure: Jump him. It's the only way to find out. But I bet if you have to jump him to get anything out of him, he's just too blasé about it, so prepare yourself for embarrassment. Still, at least you won't be wondering what would or should or could have happened after the 3 a.m. concert or the LP session.

13

Why does he engage in pointless pursuit?

THE AARON FILES

There are game players and there are game players. The former, in case it is unclear, is the type that enjoys messing with your mind once you're already dating. Treat 'em mean, keep 'em keen and all that. It can be hard to resist these dudes, as we all know (you always want what you can't quite have). The second type is rarer and, once you've spotted what he's up to, is simply too lame for words. It's just that spotting one can take a little while and before you know it you've wasted valuable energy on a dead end. And though the reality is these guys are lame-arses, they do beg a niggling question: why do they bother to lead you on and flirt with you and act all interested when they don't even want a date? What's with the dead end?

THE CASE

I met Aaron through friends at a dinner party. The second I clapped eyes on him I thought, 'Interesting, but no way am I going there.' He was far too full of himself: good-looking and he clearly knew it. Guys like that are never good news. All the same, I thought it would be amusing (OK, really nice) if this definition of tall, dark and handsome turned his eye on me despite my cynical froideur. It would be a bit like Mr Darcy and Lizzie Bennet. Lo and behold, the more I shunned him, the more Aaron became attentive towards me. By the end of dinner, we were flirting like mad – his fault, not mine. Still, I had to assume it was firmly in the realms of friendly banter: I'm not the Californian cheerleader lookalike this kind of guy usually goes for. He was also a little thick, in that sports-mad, blokey-bloke way of some guys. So I took the piss and he took the piss back and at the end of the night, though we'd bantered non-stop, I didn't think anything more of it.

Imagine my surprise when our mutual friend told me a few days later that Aaron had thought I was 'really sexy'. Well, I thought, maybe opposites do attract: maybe dumb blondes do get old for a guy like him. Somehow we started to bump into each other at dinners and parties. Since I knew what he thought about me, I couldn't help but flirt a little less innocently. He knew I knew what he had said too, and upped his flirtation. Nothing happened, but he became increasingly explicit, asking me about the kind of guys I like and whether I'd ever consider someone like him. 'OK,' I thought, 'a protracted build-up.' It would make our inevitable hook-up all the better.

We exchanged numbers and I started getting flirtatious emails from Aaron. He was hitting on me from all sides – apart from actually asking me out. Weeks passed and it seemed that we'd reached a plateau. I got bored. Then, at a friend's birthday, I decided enough was enough. I fancied a snog, and made that clear. As I did so, he backed away, responding to my virtually upturned face with something seemingly better: a question about my weekend plans. This was a first: he was finally ready to move from fruitless banter to a date. I said I wasn't sure, and waited for him to call.

I heard nothing, and on Sunday I was out having drinks locally with some friends when I decided to text him: did he fancy popping out for one? No, he replied, he was feeling lazy and was going to stay in watching the football.

I was annoyed, but felt vindicated too. He'd proved my initial suspicions were correct: studmuffins are trouble. He was certainly all talk and no action, but the situation was definitely odd. He'd flirted with me for months, made like he was going to kiss me at any second, finally asked me out (sort of), then chucked it all away without so much as making the effort to come out for a single drink. Why would a guy do that? Is it fear? Laziness? Guile? Surely he had better things to do than pursue me without any intention of even snogging me? He knew I didn't take him that seriously, so the chances of my getting attached too quickly were slim. I really couldn't make it out. He'd been the initiator after all. And it annoyed me that he left me feeling wrong-footed.

WHAT THE GUYS THINK

JOHN F, 32, IN A SERIOUS RELATIONSHIP

John is a Class A explainer of male behaviour, having been a rogue but who is now a decent, heroic boyfriend. He's not sympathetic to game players like Aaron.

Perfect for the trophy cabinet

'Aaron is clearly a narcissist. He craves female attention; he needs to be liked, loved or fancied – or preferably all three. For a guy like this, the bleached blonde, perma-tanned wag-wannabes are no longer a prize. They're easy prey. You, on the other hand, represent something entirely different. You're intelligent and, dare I say, probably a bit of a feminist (but not in a dungaree, hirsute kind of way), which makes you perfect for Aaron's trophy cabinet.

'Blokes like Aaron believe they can pull any girl – from the pointlessly vacuous, to the seriously sharp. But to prove it every now and again he needs to get under the skin – but not necessarily under the sheets – with a girl like you. He's playing you: his game is to get you to like him, to lust after him, to fuel his uncontrollable ego. But there was only ever going to be a finite period of time before he got bored and moved on.

'Don't get me wrong, I'm sure he enjoyed the texts and steamy banter – I dare say it would have even turned him on – but the truth is, Aaron is only ever going to care about one thing: himself.'

Evidently he was so concerned with the ego boost of making me like him, the physical side of it was barely on his mind (plus he'd probably had his share of shagging and wasn't gagging for it). But take comfort: all does not end well for guys like Aaron. The word 'comeuppance' springs to mind.

Nothing without his looks

'There is good news. Aaron's halcyon days of being the biggest swinging dick in town are numbered. I know guys like Aaron only too well. And like wine that comes in a plastic two-litre bottle, they don't age well. And they know they are nothing without their looks. Worse still, receding hairlines and boob flab make these guys borderline suicidal. They do settle down eventually, and shack up with a pretty, vacuous girl from Surrey with an eating disorder. But their marriage is loveless, their life soulless. And their kids will be too juiced up on cocaine and cannabis to know that their parents are days away from a messy divorce.

'The Aarons of this world need the texts and banter to fuel their egos and flood their insecurities. My advice: don't go there, unless you want to end up frustrated. He is programmed to only ever do one thing and walk away. But maybe you should also ask yourself whether it would really have felt any better if he went on the date?'

So

He's a one-trick pony: it's all about the trophy cabinet. To make it into the cabinet, all you have to do is show you're interested. That's the nugget of assurance his ego craves. Don't even bother with a guy like this, at least not until he's older and uglier, which is when his arrogance might fade.

JON B, 28, SINGLE

Jon is partial to a clever lady, and he's anything but the dumb-blonde-chaser. He can see why a guy like Aaron might be piqued by – but not want to get to actual date stage with – a woman who's smarter than his usual type.

Strange, sexy wordsmith

'You definitely offered him something he was unused to. He was excited by you not only because of your quicksilver charm, but because you pushed him to the limits of his own articulacy and wit. It was this that made you distinctive from the girls he was used to. But this was probably also the reason that it was never going to go anywhere. Because if you got more physical, he would not see you as this strange, sexy wordsmith but instead compare you on a superficial level to his stock-in-trade.'

Enjoyably verbal realm

'His avoidance of the kiss in favour of hypothetical weekend planning was surely an attempt to keep your relationship purely in the enjoyably verbal realm. I also think that his failure to come for a drink was probably down to a lack of self-confidence. Being isolated with a girl of your ilk and her friends is a great opportunity to impress, but if the guy was, as you say, "a little thick", there was the potential to look at best boring and at worst stupid.'

So

Intelligence and wit can be interesting to a guy in a way they think, at first, is sexual. It's something new and challenging – it's a slice of a more interesting world, it's something out of the ordinary. But as soon as the prospect of a physical consummation appears – even if it's just a kiss with potential – this sort of guy realizes how he was straying into a realm he doesn't want to enter. He finds the intelligence temporarily alluring, but wants to keep it at arm's length, since it's not something he sees himself getting mixed up in or turned on by.

BOTTOM LINE

If you're witty and clever (and maybe a little confrontational), you'll be familiar with the kind of sparky, sexy interchange your brain can land you in with guys. But for good-looking meatheads like Aaron, that interchange can be just a little too dangerous. They like to play with fire, to push the boat out, but they don't want to jump into the fire (or the boat). Some guys just prefer banter without action: it works for their egos, their amusement and their laziness. Superior intelligence in a woman is a particularly sensitive issue for the male ego and may be a reason for keeping a relationship at banter level, i.e. safe and controlled. Yet again, ladies, a tale of ego-bashing by our scary smarts (see also the Raphael Files in Chapter 12 and the Michael Files in Chapter 20).

What to do if you still want that date: Go back to square one and totally back off. Of course, once he feels the trophy is walking out of his cabinet, he'll return for more – after all, it's not good enough that you're only interested in him for five seconds, you have to stay interested. It'll be texts and emails again, which you'll need to keep cool about. Then it's a waiting game. Don't even think about suggesting a date. Eventually, your aloofness will get to him, and he'll ask. To be on the safe side, you might want to stand him up on the first one.

14

Why does sex kill all the interest?

THE LASSE FILES

It's just taken as fact that women get attached when they have sex and men don't. There is obviously a spectrum of female and male behaviour, but you'd be hard pressed to find anyone who thought this rule was reversed – although maybe Samantha from *Sex and the City* would. But here's the thing. You hear a lot about how men always want sex. You grow up hearing that kind of thing. So something has always niggled me: the numerous times I've experienced or heard about men completely losing interest after one single measly shag.

Now, you might say it's because they don't want you to get the wrong idea about anything more serious happening. But that is not what I'm talking about. I am talking about a guy you meet, say, on a weekend break abroad and shag. You're leaving two days later. You're exciting because you're new and wild. And still, one shag and he's out of there. The best you can hope for the next day is some non-committal text-flirting, certainly not a 'please can I see you again before you leave, pretty please?' Not a trace of that fervent drink-buying, bed-luring man from the day before.

What's going on? Is it literally that a guy doesn't want to sleep with the same girl twice, even though there is no way in hell she'll get clingy? Does sex really murder all interest in a woman – unless, of course, there's something more long term on the cards? If so, what has happened to the idea that men are big old sex monsters who'll take what they can get? After all, whenever I've met a guy who is clearly only after a mini-fling, and who I only want as a mini-fling too, I make it obvious that he can have me, without any strings. But no. Not having it. Why not? What happens to that famous libido when a girl is up for a little more of the same?

THE CASE

I was on holiday in Berlin recently. It was a Friday night – we were there till Sunday. My friend Anna and I were sitting in a bar sipping some vodka tonics and wondering what to do with ourselves next, when a couple of guys started looking at us. Next thing we knew, some shots of tequila arrived in front of us. The waitress pointed out our benefactors and we had to smile – they were cute.

The ringleader, Lasse, seemed extremely unsleazy and gave the impression of enjoying the tourist-guide role. He offered to show us a few of his favourite Berlin nightspots, and we said yes. The first place we headed was a weird punk venue playing such gems as Green Day. I went up to the bar and some guy started talking to me. Lasse was there in a minute, and ushered me away jealously – he was clearly keen.

Nothing happened, apart from us bopping around a fair bit, and soon Lasse herded us on to the next place, a famous Berlin bar called Delicious Donuts. We were drunk now, and tired. The three of us slouched on a sofa and chatted and laughed and eventually, around

4 a.m., it was time to go. We all jumped in a cab – Lasse wanted to see us home – and we exchanged numbers.

Anna and I had just got to our room when I got a text: 'You could be in my arms within minutes . . .' It was cheesy as hell, yet there was something so sexy about this message that I put my coat right back on and headed out to meet him. It was 5 a.m., but who cared? When we met he had a tulip in his hand for me – another killing touch. His flat was all thick wood-panelled floors and minimalist whitewash, with all the gadgets a self-respecting bachelor should have. He poured me a glass of good wine, put on some music, and kissed me as I looked out the window at the amazing view. We snogged for a decent amount of time before jumping into bed. The sex was good, but because we were both so tired and drunk, it wasn't perfect. I sneaked off while he lay there snoring.

The next day I decided to leave it, not wanting to appear too keen, but assuming he'd be in touch. At around 3 p.m., as Anna and I were lying on top of the Bundestag, he texted something both flirtatious and non-committal, and asked about our plans later.

That night, as Anna and I sat in another trendy bar, we rather missed Lasse. I wasn't averse to having another go at last night's drunken effort either, so I texted to tell him where we were. No reply. I realized some of my texts had stopped sending in Germany – something to do with my rubbish network – and I became convinced this friendly guy hadn't replied not because he'd suddenly gone off the idea of playing host and having more sex, but because my phone simply hadn't sent the message.

So I texted from Anna's phone. When there was still no reply, it dawned on me that he was either asleep or really not up for it. Much later, he replied, to my phone (he'd got the message after all), saying that he was tired and hoped we'd have a good night. Ouch. Ouch. Ouch.

So we had a few more drinks, me feeling deeply embarrassed, and we went to bed early.

Before getting on the plane the next day, Lasse texted me something cheesy, about how he'd been happy he'd got the chance to meet me, had enjoyed our time together and that he'd be looking me up next time he was in London. I scornfully didn't reply. The next week I wrote my column about guys who get scared off and put up the barriers after just one hook-up when the girl's leaving the next day anyway. Early onset commitment phobia. Lasse read it (hello, Google), and texted a long, joke-wounded text about how he'd been genuinely tired.

But come on – tiredness is a pathetic excuse. I was tired too! Or are some guys so unbothered about getting laid they'll go off the idea because they're a little worn out? On the second night he acted like he was afraid of getting roped into something, though he knew it wasn't a possibility. Maybe the effort of going through it again didn't hold a candle to his laziness. But if that was the case, why had he gone to so much effort the night before, and why had he continued texting and flirting? WHAT WAS THE POINT? Did sex just poison all interest in me?

WHAT THE GUYS THINK

VICTOR L, 28, IN A SERIOUS RELATIONSHIP

Victor has been known to mime a line graph to explain the difference between male and female orgasms. He's that clued up about how men experience sex differently from women.

Bam, it's gone

'That's men all over. There's a big build-up, then you just want one night, not two. It's like the difference between male and female orgasms: men come and then lust drops suddenly; with women it falls more slowly.

'The excitement was built up throughout that first night, then bam, it's gone. It's not like he loved you. And after sex, a guy couldn't be less horny: He just wants to spend a few nights with his boys. The whole of the first night he's thinking, "I gotta shag her" – but once it's done, it's done.'

Here's a clue to the next issue. It begins with a *c*.

'If you're acting all keen for a follow-up, where's the chase? If a beautiful girl comes up to you and says, "You're gorgeous, let's have sex at mine", you'll find her less attractive than a girl who is not as pretty, but who you've had to work hard for.'

Once again I was the keen bean. It comes up again and again: nothing – but nothing – puts a guy off more than keenness (see the quick-fire question on page 34).

So

A man's interest plummets dramatically after sex and this lasts until there's time for a chase to build up again. He'd rather do anything but see you again shortly after he's shagged you. His desire has to return from a zero, while ours just bubbles away in a slightly more complex low-level emotional zone. Being keen and available, as I was with Lasse, is the surest method to keep him away.

LEWIS L, 29, SINGLE

A trendy young bachelor who tries hard to impress women, Lewis sympathizes with the desire to have an easy night in.

Prefer an early night

'It's a mistake to think that guys are always up for it. I personally sometimes prefer having an early night than going out. A guy needs to be ready to fight when he goes out. It requires a lot of work to be funny, open, smiley, confident, etc., and despite all of that you can be sure that someone at some point during the night will reject you. Most of the time you are ready to take the risk, but if you feel a bit low, it's sometimes better to stay home than have a rubbish night.

'Maybe Lasse had a busy week and was up for a big one on Friday

night but just wanted to chill out on Saturday. If you are tired you
are not going to answer a booty call. Every time I've done that, it's
been crap. To really enjoy this kind of one-off relationship you need
to quickly create a high level of sexual tension, which requires lots
of energy, or you face the risk that the mayonnaise doesn't thicken
– I don't know if you have ever made a mayonnaise, but if you
don't whisk it properly it very quickly turns into a useless gloopy
glutinous lump.'

I've never made mayonnaise, but I know what he means.

So

Sometimes men just feel like being lazy hermits instead of going into
the sexual battlefields. At home, or with mates, nothing much can go
wrong. Out with women, there are plenty of hits and downers to bear.
Keeping the mayonnaise smooth is hard work. Who knew?

IAIN H, 29, SINGLE

Iain is a player, a charmer and a holiday-romance aficionado. He knows
all the rules and tricks. He also thinks it's blatantly obvious that sleeping with the same girl twice is infinitely less preferable to a one-nighter.

Like two weddings on consecutive nights

'Your problem with Lasse was that he was a one-night stand – and it's
called "one night" for a reason. In this case, you're attempting to find
some sort of non-existent middle ground between a proper holiday
romance and a wham-bam-thank-you-ma'am. You've fallen between
two stools. Hard. After the first night Lasse had got all that he wanted:
the thrill of the (long) chase, the excitement of the conquest and a
story for his mates. The next evening would only be the same, but
worse, like trying to go to two weddings on consecutive nights. Plus,
he was probably feeling embarrassed about being such a poor, snoring
lover (or he had a girlfriend). The same would apply to you at home if

you met a guy at a party or a club and had a one-night stand. You're just some girl who may be perfectly lovely – but you're still just a girl – and once a guy has had his dirty drunken sex with you, there is no reason he would make an effort to repeat, or try to recreate, that experience. In general, for men, a one-night stand is always just that.'

Dumpable offence

'You don't need me to point out that repeated texting from multiple phones is not particularly cool or that Lasse's "friendly" desire to show you his favourite Berlin nightspots was merely a mask for his evident desire to ply you with alcohol and jump you.'

Well, yes.

'But cheer up: I think you've probably had a lucky escape. A guy who's unable to make a move in a bar, a nightclub or a cab but texts you a message so trite that, even if it were lost in Germanic trans-lation, it would still count as an instantly dumpable offence? A guy who suddenly produces a tulip at 5 a.m.? (Was this one of his "self-respecting" bachelor gadgets?) A guy who didn't even have the decency to attempt a threesome with your friend? No, I'd leave Lasse in the doghouse where he belongs.'

What sound advice. Iain is sort of saying that Lasse is an embar-rassed geek, exhausted after his not totally successful efforts in the sack – but also that, like Victor said, the appeal of round two is never strong.

So

The last thing Lasse wanted after fulfilling his goal of sex – and then doing it badly – was another round. He was depleted. Finished. And probably a little embarrassed. Of course, it didn't help that I'd texted him from multiple phones.

BOTTOM LINE

Unless they're totally in love with you, guys are never, ever going to be up for it the very next night. I was a fool to even suggest it, repelling him even more. This is down to two things. One: guys lose interest after one shag. For them it's case closed, been there, got the T-shirt, got the biscuit, etc. Two (and again this is mainly a factor when the feelings aren't strong): guys get tired and can, indeed actually prefer, laying low or going out with their mates to sex. Have your Friday night sex, but know the last thing he wants will be Saturday night sex – with you.

What to do if you want to sleep with Mr One-Night Stand again: Lay low, and wait till you can reasonably bump into him again without it seeming arranged. Or, if he's from abroad or out of town, when he visits your neck of the woods, the chances are he'll give you a bell. You have to become a fresh idea again – remember Victor's line graph. Men have to work up to it from zero, and you become a zero on the desire scales after you sleep with him. My advice is: there's a special little Lasse for everyone in any city at any time. Just exchange him for the next one. Now that's real tourism.

15

Why does he go off you as soon as you take it from friends that fancy each other to actual girlfriend and boyfriend?

THE CHARLIE FILES

I used to believe that the man I married would start out as a best friend. In fact, I used to not be able to help myself from fancying all my close male friends. They know you well, you know them, they're lovely to you, you spend a lot of time alone together having a whale of a time, you have so much in common and they're really rather cute. However, my oft-considered fantasy of becoming more than friends with the several male mates I've fancied never really happened – for me, things have always developed from a physical beginning.

But that's just me. My own experience doesn't change my view that going from friends to lovers seems like the absolute best possible part of every world. I've seen it work and, when I do, part of me has to keep my tongue from hanging out and drooling with a kind of perverse jealousy.

But weirdly, I've also seen it fail a lot. I've seen BFs get together, be inseparable for a while, then lose everything (friendship first and foremost) when it all goes tits up after a few months or so.

What's interesting is that the reason it goes tits up is generally a problem on the guy's side. He might spend every night in his best female friend's bed when they're not an item, but as soon as they are, he goes off her and can't cope.

How come?

THE CASE

My mate Charlotte, a cute and bubbly vet, had become friends with Charlie in their second year of university. They met through a larger circle that moved as a pack, but these two eventually became the staple. They were inseparable.

After we all came to London, the group stayed pretty close. Charlotte and Charlie both saw other people but spent the rest of their time together – literally. It was a common occurrence for one to crash in the other's bed after a night out together (of which there were many). Neither seemed to take the other's relationships seriously, and from the outside perspective, as well as Charlotte's, they loved each other – even if it was just platonically – more than they could love anyone else. Charlotte definitely saw Charlie's girlfriends as interlopers, bits of fluff that couldn't really compete with her.

The other thing was their physicality. Now, most friends don't kiss on the lips or cuddle each other or sleep spooning each other. These guys did. It was like a freaky mixture of best friends, brother and sister, and people who really, really wanted to have sex with each other.

Throughout most of this, both vigorously denied that they fancied each other.

But then, after a couple of years in which she couldn't make any other relationship work, Charlotte began confessing to her friends that she fancied Charlie. That confession soon became that she was in love with Charlie.

At around this time, it seemed that things had to come to a head: the inseparability, the bed-sharing, the lip-kissing and even a one-off snog had gone too far. And, lo and behold, they got together and decided to be a couple. Charlotte was in heaven. I had assumed Charlie must have been too. I was waiting for the wedding invitation.

But then, a mere three months later, Charlie started talking about not being ready, or sure, and all those excuses people use when they just aren't into it/you. Whereas he couldn't spend enough time with Charlotte when they were friends, he began looking for ways out. Charlotte was heartbroken, her life's dream seemingly shattered; and, although Charlotte was willing to try anything to stay together with Charlie, he broke it off a short time later.

He's now in a relationship with another woman and Charlotte's recovered but hasn't really moved on. They spend very little time together these days.

What happened? Why is it that when a guy seems to be in love with his female friend and vice versa, actually being in a relationship turns him off her entirely? Was it that he saw her as more of a mother/sister with the convenience of the non-related vagina? Did their closeness ultimately make it impossible to fancy her because she lacked mystique? Was she just a crutch to his ego? Why, when it seemed like a match made in heaven with his tried and tested soulmate, did Charlie break it off?

WHAT THE GUYS THINK

MARCUS F, 28, SINGLE
Marcus is a romantic, and very choosy about who he goes out with since he wants everything to be perfect. He reckons the fairy tale of best friends getting together is overwhelming for guys, whereas we just want that fairy tale to happen asap.

Pressure

'The BF get-together is a beautiful play, but one with high stakes. I would say this particular failure was probably down to one thing: pressure. Now I know what you are thinking, this is a pretty tired cliché about men and responsibility and commitment, and there have been roughly 2,000 uninspired jokes about it on twenty-/thirty-something sitcoms since for ever, but it is true.'

That's right: you can't coax a man into a committed relationship. The more right you and it seem, the scarier it is to him. Softly-softly is the necessary approach.

The big dilemma

'I think Charlie genuinely loved Charlotte, and it sounds like proper fairy-tale soulmate stuff too. I guess he slowly realized over the years that "yes, I love this woman, so why the hell aren't we together". But his epiphanic moment is blighted by a massive caveat: if this works, amazing; if it doesn't, I lose everything. Thus lies the dilemma of the BF get-together.'

'Shit, I've got to marry her'

'So, the obvious became inevitable. The sexual tension, unbearable. And the two get together. Neurosis being what it is, I'm guessing the first thing to cross Charlie's mind after the post-coital haze subsided was, "Shit, I've pretty much got to marry her now." From your description, this was a pretty big deal for Charlotte. We are talking "life's dream" big, which is major. This instantly puts supreme pressure on a relationship that was already pretty complicated.'

Pressure, ladies. Pressure is a one-way street in matters of the heart – we're the ones who take it. We're not allowed to put it on, whether we mean to or not.

Sad, slow disaster

'There is no grace period/getting-to-know-you stage – this thing has to work, and it has to work straight away. Yes, they are already best friends, but if someone looks you in the eye and says, "I'm relying on you/this relationship for my life's happiness", that can be hard to handle (and this doesn't usually happen within the first month of a relationship). So if there is even a flicker of doubt in Charlie's mind (or Charlotte's) then it won't work. Combine that doubt with the rock-solid certainty of the other's love, and the result is a sad, slow disaster.'

So

The apparent perfection of getting together with your super-close friend – the perfection that makes us desperate to do it – seems to guys like a marriage contract they're not sure they can or want to live up to. The moment you get together, because you are already necessarily serious, there is no opportunity to let the relationship build slowly. That important time of letting the relationship develop is bypassed. This only adds to the sense of being overwhelmed – and, for a guy, nothing's more of a relationship-killer than that.

NATHAN D, 30, IN A RELATIONSHIP

Nathan, who has been in some very serious relationships, spots a hell of a lot of reasons why the friend-to-lover thing freaks guys out. As usual, the issues tend to be about ego and control, safety and fear. Also, guys want everything: the clever woman who is devoted to nurturing him, but is also deeply alluring and smelling of roses (see the Michael Files in Chapter 20). They want the friend at home adoring them while they go off and attempt to get it on with other women. You're the safe bet and the safety net.

Safety net – other women

'Basically the problem here is that the allure of *the chase* is lost. Starting out as friends is fine because a level of sexual tension and possibility is maintained. The girl-as-friend is in a sense a safety net for Charlie, which allows him to go off and pursue other women while also maintaining the maternal-stay-at-home mumsy desire all guys have and need. Having the girl-as-friend is allowing the guy to have his cake and eat it too. He basically has the friend as potential lover/partner where he wants her – *he* remains in control.

'It's also the perfect Madonna-and-whore split: Madonna at home, side by side in bed, snuggling up, and then there's the chasing after other women. The latter is made more "stable" in the guy's head because he knows he has the friend to come back to at night for intimacy if the other pursuits should fail, or if the guy is rejected. Long-term friendships that have the potential to become fully fledged relationships also have a lot to live up to because both parties have at some point contemplated the idea and then had to put it in the back of their minds. But the potential has always been there, which is important, because there is a slow build-up of possibility and expectation, at least on the part of the woman, who finally stakes her claim for Charlie.'

Yep, slow build-up, followed by an intense detonation.

Upsets apple cart

When Charlotte announces her intentions she is basically saying, 'I want to take over and steer this where it's going – I want more.' For Charlie, who may have considered it and clearly likes keeping the possibility open, suddenly there's pressure and so he simply steps back and thinks it's weird. The intimacy they had as friends was good precisely because the balance between friend/partner was so well adjusted. Charlotte upset the balance.

So

The tacit agreement that they might get together, that they could get together, but that they weren't getting together, was what the whole chemistry in this friendship was based on. It was never meant to be a real relationship, because what kept the whole prospect alluring and piquant was the sense of possibility. Once it was realized, and became reality, the fact that they were friends to begin with – not lovers – became an important, obvious fact. That is, they were never meant to go out – in Charlie's mind, that is. Also, guys can't merge mother (Charlotte) with whore (other women) so easily. While every woman's dream man is a combination of her father and a sex stud/romantic dreamboat, a guy would not fancy a woman (consciously) that fulfilled mothering needs for him. And Charlotte did just that.

BOTTOM LINE

There are tons of reasons friend-to-lover relationships fail. They are almost doomed to fail, because as both guys were at pains to explain, the pressure of fulfilling a fairy tale is a killer. Then there's the fact that he might fail to find you, his friend, sexy since he knows you so well and there's no chase – remember: the chase is all-important for a lot of guys. Or he might find his attraction to you (after all, you did get together) was based on not yet being with you, that little bit of mystery and the sense of possibility. Finally, he may even prefer you as the doting friend: it allows him to go off into the sexual wilds knowing he has adoring old you at home. And if making you dote on him means a little lip kissing and spooning here and there, well, that's a price he's more than willing to pay. More fool you. This might be a good time to turn to the Mark Files in Chapter 11 for comment/inspiration on pulling out when you're not getting what you want from a man.

What to do if you fancy your friend: Don't go there if you suspect you want it more than he does. If both hearts are pounding, it's fine; if one is beating faster than the other, there will be big problems. Marcus recommends 'a cautious passion'. After what these guys have said, it seems to me like the only option is to let him come to you, and even when he does, it can't hurt to play hard to get, to make him convince himself he *really* wants it. As we've seen, the faintest doubt leads to disaster because the guy knows it has to be for ever or never. Ladies, the chase is never obsolete! That's not to say that if you've fallen in love with your friend that you need to suffer in silence. You may be able to awaken his passion, you just need to do it the right way. If you're the gorgeous one and he's less so, a bit of suggestive dressing and confidence might do it. If it's not quite like that, see the quick-fire question on page 279 about how guys feel when their friends fancy them. It's not the most encouraging. That is, they rarely think, 'Wow, maybe I fancy this amazing person too. What a turn-on that this great friend fancies me.' No, it's more, 'Oh shit, what do I do now?'

Quick-fire questions 4

Have you ever knowingly strung a girl along and if so, why?

This is a huge and important subject that touches on mixed signals and commitment phobia too. That's why I've included so many of the guys' answers below. I think it's deliciously interesting as it explains all that unspoken weirdness that leaves you waiting for the phone to ring when you were sure they'd be in touch. Mostly they string us along because we let them – we give them sex and desperately want to believe that this will bring something with it. That's because we like them and it's always easy to nurture hopes based on very little. Anyway, there are several big reasons guys do it – read on.

NADAV H: 'Of course. There are so many reasons. One: sometimes you're not sure if you want it and you need some time to think about it. During that time, you may have to look a bit more excited than you really are, so as not to insult the other side and, of course, to keep your options open. Two: some people (like me) just hate being alone. I guess that we haven't got enough confidence to feel that the world likes us without a little help from our (female) friends. So we need them, and sometimes it looks like we are developing emotions even when we aren't. We just hate being alone. Three: sex, of course – although, with the way that we (men) are built, it's never the main reason. That's because usually after two or three times with one girl, we start thinking about others. Four: company. I remember keeping something going only because there was a rock festival in the south of Israel at the end of that week and I wanted someone to go with. Five: making an ex feel jealous.'

DANIEL F: 'Yes, for sex. Are you going to give up sex because a girl asks you if you like them and you say, "Not that much"? No way.'

KOBI N: 'Yes I have, for many reasons: the sex could be good or because it feels good to be wanted even though I know that the relationship is not right for me and isn't going anywhere.'

AARON B: 'Yes. If you're already sleeping with someone, the promise of a permanent relationship, even if you don't envisage one, has the practical benefit that you get more sex. Then there is the case where you continually flirt with someone whom you have no interest in but who is evidently into you. That can be very pleasant.'

ROB M: 'Yes, it can be a very gratifying ego boost to lead someone on and be sure you have it in the bag without having to follow through; this has been a motive for me at times of low self-esteem. Sometimes, it's genuine confusion, generally on my part, as to what constitutes efforts to build a friendship with a girl and what comes across as romantic advances. I like to think that some of the weeping maidens I have left in my trail have been victims of this innocent misunderstanding, though I realize that in most if not all cases there has been an element of deliberate leading on there too.'

Have you ever gone off a girl between dates two and three? Or, for that matter, for no apparent reason?

TIM M: 'Loads of times. Sometimes it can be the silliest of reasons that put you off, such as a strange comment or if she smokes, etc. It just means you weren't that into them in the first place but you fancied getting your leg over. Shit, we're men after all.'

MARK F: 'Yes. When I was young I used to go to discos and occasionally I would manage to snog a girl. I usually found that I went off them immediately after or during [!] the snog. This may have seemed to them like I was going off them for no apparent reason, but I think the actual reason was that I was never really sufficiently keen on them and the experience of actually being with them – and the sensation of bad faith that came with it – brought that home to me. I found the experience of being with someone I wasn't completely keen on so uncomfortable that I resolved at an early stage not to go out with people unless I was completely keen.'

DENNIS D: 'Yes. Often. Here's why. A big difference between men and women is the matter of confidence or, if you like, form. As a chap you spend your time in, or at least feeling like you're in, great peaks or troughs of form. Consequently,

what quite often happens is that instead of meeting one
girl, getting along or not, and then moving on to another if
not, instead you meet two (or more) at the same time and
a decision's made after you've had a bit of time with both
of them. Then there's the fact that one date is nowhere
near enough time to expose cracks and flaws – anyone
with an ounce of social skills can be interesting, witty and
maybe even vivacious for a night. Second time around
there's a chance that those cracks get brutally exposed; I
think on the whole men are more likely to take a chance
and then decide "Nah", whereas women tend not to
bother in the first place unless they think there's something there and so they'll stick around for longer to see
how it goes.'

Can a guy be best friends with a girl without any physical attraction at all?

Now, this isn't conclusive. But in a funny way both add up to the same
thing: there can be 'friend' modes that are rigid – the idea is fixed in
each party's head from the start. But every now and again they slide
around a bit, though usually at different times.

TIM V: 'No. There will always have been something somewhere at some point, but it can be conflicted, temporary
and also fades over time. Only when you see someone as a
sister-figure or your friend's "property" can you manage
never to see them sexually. But when circumstances
change, so can your feelings.'

FREDDIE W: 'No. You can have the friendship but the
possibility of sex is always on both parties' minds at some
point, usually at different points. This doesn't have to

interfere, especially as the feeling or thought often comes up randomly and goes away quickly, depending on what else is going on in your life of course.'

Would the possibility of ruining the friendship stop you sleeping with/getting fully involved with a friend?

Note that the short answer is always yes, 'because I didn't fancy her enough'. But the long answers below are equally illuminating.

ALAN W: 'Yes. Well, it has done and has probably worked out for the best in that we still talk. I thought whether they would be long-term relationship material and then whether having sex with someone else was a better approach than potentially wrecking a friendship. I have also been caught in a bind between someone who could be a friend (and an interesting one at that) and could be a lover/girlfriend. We ended up in bed but she didn't want anything more than kisses because, I think, she was looking for sufficient confirmation that I would be back the next week and the week after. I wasn't. Friends can tolerate periods of silence; girlfriends cannot.'

TOM A: 'Yes. What gets confusing in male/female relationships is when one half goes through a phase and gets all sad and blue about life and starts looking for quick routes to happiness, which often manifests as seeing how great the chum is, and therefore how great a partner they would make. Usually you're wrong, and even if you get as far as saying or trying to do something, they gently put you right. And all is well. But then if you both happen to have those same blue thoughts at the same time, a world of confusion begins and that can become a world of trouble. And then you have the bald fact that you can be friends with someone for years and years and not sleep with them thousands of times, but do it just once and that's it: you once slept together and that means that you could do it again.'

GEORGE L: 'Erm, it has done, but mainly because I wasn't as in love with the girl as she was with me. Luckily we're still friends now; I doubt it would have remained that way if we'd given the relationship a go. I think that guys have to know they practically want to marry the girl before they plunge in from friendship. It's too much of a dive off the deep end otherwise.'

Has it ever happened that a girl seemed attractive to you until you saw her naked?

Now, almost everyone I asked about this said no. Here's the standout yes. It's chilling, and, thankfully, I think an exception. But it's honest. And is it any different from us discovering a penis we don't like and running for the hills?

BEN F: 'Yes. I once went out with a girl who was from Montreal. She had exquisite features: dark exotic eyes and ruby red lips. She wasn't skinny, or overweight, just curvy. We make it back to my place and clothes just start flying off in every direction. Then I see it! Stretch marks galore! It was like someone twisted up this girl's body in a bunch and never undid it. She had fat in all the wrong places, those perfectly accented curves looked like the size of icebergs, and her tits, which looked so voluptuous and perky under her V-neck sweater, now were nothing more than deflated balloons. That ruined it for me completely.

After that I completely lost interest. I decided to go with it for the night and let her feel like she was getting what she wanted. After that, I never called her again. Now it is clear to me that clothes play funny tricks on you.'

How important is it to a guy that a woman is thin? Do you prefer superthin or curvy – perhaps even plump – women?

NOAH A: 'If we want to seem nice, we'll tell you, "No, no – I don't like those model types. I don't want to shag a girl who looks unhealthy." While deep-down we'll be convinced that we'd pick any thin girl over a curvy one. But we're lying to ourselves. Who we think we're attracted to is far more influenced by depictions in media of feminine beauty than who we're actually attracted to. So we're honestly, genuinely convinced that we'd always pick the thin girl over the curvy girl. But it's just not true.

I've done a little poll among my friends: "Which features are most important to you? Face, boobs, bum, legs?" Nobody said it was the face. But when I watch them at a party or at a bar or choosing between potential girlfriends, it's always the girl with the pretty face who ultimately wins out. So, notionally, it's all-important for us that a woman is thin. In reality, it's not. If you're curvy and pretty, don't you worry. The only time when your boy will wish that you were thinner is when he's talking to his mates – or deluding himself.'

BEN F: 'Every guy has a different idea of their perfect woman. Some guys are all about the tits. They want them big, small, perky, round, fat, white, black, yellow, etc. Some guys are all about the bum. And some guys are even into the eyes. I personally don't find it important for a girl to be thin. If a girl is larger and takes care of herself, then we are good. It's the girls who play the natural card and say, "This is what I was given and I am going to accept it and that's that!" I HATE THOSE GIRLS! If you are heavily overweight, jump on the treadmill, stopping eating cookies for breakfast, have some portion control and take care of your body.'

Clearly, Ben needs to chill out a little. But I still think he is giving a fairly typical male view – a very superficial, slightly porno one, but a common enough one. He's not the only one who's talked about 'taking care' of ourselves. Obviously there's something repellent in the idea of someone who has 'let themselves go' – even though plenty of men seem to do it with impunity.

ANTHONY R: 'I'm a fan of thin girls but I have dated different sizes. I used to be a huge fan of very thin girls but have become more partial to curvy ones over the years. I still prefer thin but not bony thin. As for plump, I'm at the age now where I am thinking long term, where plump may turn to obese. I would tend to shy away from that now. I am living in Korea where all the girls are thin, and it's great. So yeah, I would say thin-curvy, but not plump. This is for relationships of course. Plump sex is lovely.'

How important is a woman's grooming, i.e. hair removal, highlights, pedicures, etc., to you?

A lot of women spend a lot of time and money trying to figure this out. That's why I've devoted so much space to the guys' answers. Justin's reply, the third, is extensive, but I think worthwhile. Paul offers some great advice if you're worried about your grooming, or unconvinced by the cost and pain of maintaining the illusion of being a hairless wonder. See the second half of his answer. But in general, they don't ask too much. Their absolute no-nos are pretty basic, like don't have stinking feet or a hairy face.

PAUL E: 'At a basic level, grooming is crucial. I could not be involved with someone who didn't wash properly or clean their teeth. BO and bad breath are enormous turn-offs. Personally I find women who over-groom, i.e. who wear too much make-up, have garishly dyed hair, bright nail varnish, maybe even cosmetic surgery, unattractive. Some men are attracted to exactly that. There are few things I find less attractive than hair in places where it ought not to be for a woman, i.e. upper lip, sideburns. I don't find bushy eyebrows, hairy armpits, hairy legs or overgrown pubic thatches particularly attractive either. How you groom at a sophisticated level will simply determine the type of man who is attracted to you. A woman should groom in a way that she finds attractive and feels comfortable with. The ensuing confidence about the way she thinks she looks will immediately make her more attractive, and she will attract men who like her for who she is when she is at her most comfortable. It will be an authentic kind of attraction.'

Basically, everything comes down to confidence. If you feel good, guys – the right types too – will flock.

JOHN S: 'I think I have become habituated to certain things and others don't bother me. Certain things are non-negotiable for me. I once had a girlfriend with smelly feet, which was an absolute turn-off. Long term you have to

seek someone who is not high maintenance and doesn't
need to look 100 per cent at all times – they have to be
able to look after their own emotional needs and not seek
support from the outside world; I would want someone
who takes care of themselves though. So, in summary, hair
removal (not too excessive) is important, pedicures etc. are
nice and not too much make-up (I like those moments
when girlfriends don't wear any).'

JUSTIN O: 'At the start of a relationship grooming is very
important. You want to feel as attracted to them as
possible, and vice versa. However, for me these things are
always important. Hair removal: I prefer women that have
no excess hair on their faces. Even small stray ones, even
blonde small stray ones. Let's just say men in general
prefer women without hair on their faces, legs, armpits,
etc. Pubic hair: I feel this question was leading here, so I'll
just say it for the record: I prefer a Brazilian wax. Holly-
wood is too much. I thought I'd like it, then when I was
faced with it I found it a little unsettling. But the landing
strip is sexy. Is it important to me though? Well, no, it's
not. Basically, if you like someone and fancy them then
really none of this stuff matters. Also I know how much
this waxing stuff costs, and so I don't expect it all the
time. However, if you are sleeping with someone for the
first time, then I would suggest that you go for it because I
know most men do prefer a tidy lady garden.

'Manicures: not important. Doesn't even register. I
don't really look at women's nails as a judge of attractive-
ness. In fact if they are too long and polished I find it a bit
strange. Like I'm a child, and it's the eighties and I'm out
shopping with my mum, and some old crow behind the

Boots beauty counter is talking to us, and her nails are on the surface of the counter, and they are making a sort of tapping/scraping noise on the work surface, and it's hot and bright, and everything smells of perfume, and I'm tired, and this trip feels like it has lasted for three years already, and there is NOTHING here I want to look at. That kind of thing.

'Perfume: I hate it. It's too strong and overpowering. I prefer deodorant, moisturizer, etc. This all smells nice, and natural on a partner. I like my girlfriend/partner/wife to smell fragrant and natural.

'Hair: highlights are not important, but a good haircut is, and generally nice hair is a big turn-on. If a girl has nice hair then it goes a long way to getting you noticed. Well-conditioned hair is lovely, and I, like many men, love to touch women's hair, love the smell of it and just love it generally. Oh God, that makes me sound like I have a hair fetish.'

(A bit, but in a nice way.)

Have you ever thought a girl was perfect but failed to fancy her and if so, why?

THOMAS N: 'If a girl is perfect but you don't fancy her it's usually because she isn't physically what you look for. Saying that, I have been very attracted to pretty girls but once they start talking the illusion dissolves and it becomes clear there is no chemistry there. I guess alcohol is a factor that can shatter all of the above.'

PAUL N: 'I can remember saying something along the lines of, "Oh, if she only was x, or had better y or z, she would be perfect", but a long time ago. I can't remember saying anything like that recently. That's because the idea of there being a perfect woman is down to inexperience. The most important thing, first off, is to be attracted to a woman. Then, if she picks her nose, if one of her legs is shorter than the other, or she farts in bed, as long as there is that base attraction – which is as much to do with the core elements of her personality as her looks – one is not going to be dissatisfied.'

PART FIVE

Three's a Crowd

Nothing does less to keep the peace than the presence of a third party in the relationship. This section looks at three very different types of third party: a mother, a mate and another woman.

Sure, we women bring in the occasional third party: overprotective friends or parents, other men. But there's no denying the particularly strong bond between a guy and his mother, or the fact that men are up for weird sexual arrangements involving more than one woman (worry not: I've asked about threesomes in the Quick-fire section). The Sean Files in Chapter 17, in which a friend of mine found herself being hit on by her then-fling's mate, struck me as a diluted form of the threesome; it's also a tale of weird male bonding.

Intrusive mothers are an age-old problem. But when a guy in his late twenties with his own house and life seems to listen to her every word – even when it's a jibe about his girlfriend – you have to wonder just what's going on in his mind that allows him to be controlled and influenced like that. What is it about mothers anyway? Find out in the Pete Files in Chapter 16.

The Sam Files in Chapter 18 serve a dual purpose. On one hand, the story is about the lingering other girl who never goes away, and who eventually becomes the main event. But equally, it's about the incredibly exasperating fact of her inferiority. What do guys see in the dumber girl? What does she have that you – obviously closer to being his soulmate – don't have? And why do guys think it's OK to keep their options open – for months?

In the Quick-fire section we find out who would ever date their mate's ex-girlfriend and why, along with who fancies their girlfriend's friends and more.

16

Why can't he leave his mum out of his relationship?

THE PETE FILES

There's a reason the term 'mummy's boy' exists. Mummies love their boys, and boys love their mamas. Mummies cook for their boys, blow their noses for them, defend them, stroke their egos and tell them how great they are. Hell, my mother fusses over my 23-year-old brother as though he were still in nappies, fretting that he isn't eating enough and doling out seconds and thirds to him while I am merely encouraged to stay off nosh altogether.

This is all very well and good. But eventually (say, post-uni), little Johnnie should start to question his mother's role in his life, where it concerns things other than helpings of beef. He can still love her and her home-cooking, but he should see that sometimes she needs pacifying rather than heeding. She may even need to be ignored, at times.

Particularly when a special someone comes on the scene, who his mother doesn't approve of, simply because that special someone isn't her. She may concoct ways to undermine the new girlfriend, either to her face or by trying to poison sonny boy against her. But not letting her do that, recognizing that it's just Mum being nosy and jealous and neurotic, is a basic part of growing up, right?

Of course. Yet a surprising number of men (or should I say boys), with jobs, cars and houses of their own, are still completely under their mother's sway, and incapable of screening her out when she starts picking at their perfectly nice girlfriend, and possibly future wife, who does her best to please. Why?

THE CASE

Behold the difficulties faced by my friend Mira, 29, who has been going out with Pete, 30, for nine months. He still allows his mother to micro-manage his relationship with her and it's beginning to piss her off, especially as the relationship is moving at a serious pace.

Not yet grasping that it would be better if he didn't pass on to Mira his mother's every pearl of wisdom relating to her, Pete often pipes up with his mother's observations about this or that. A recent example would be her comment on the fact that Mira has let her blonde high-lights grow out, proving her theory (a nine-month-old theory, I might add: the length of the relationship) that women can't afford to take care of their appearance these days.

But the kicker came when Mira and Pete went out for a romantic evening of tapas and blues recently (she'd been away and they were celebrating her return). Just as Mira was cramming the last of the chorizo into her gob, Pete asked a little question. If they were to take things to the next step, i.e. get married, would Mira keep working or stay at home?

Whoa there. After nearly a year together, how could Pete have construed Mira as the type of girl to just give up the day job the second she secures her hubby? Much of her self-pride comes from a sense of industriousness and independence. Granted, she's not partic-ularly passionate about her job as senior support staff in a software company (she pursues a film career on the side), but she's not about to give it all up and put her feet up the second she gets married – *if* she gets married.

As she put it angrily, if you knew her, you'd understand this, and you wouldn't even think to ask the question. So where had it come from? She demanded an answer and Pete bashfully gave it.

Good old mum. She'd wanted Pete to ask, because *she* wanted to know what he was going to be up against, financially, if they tied the knot. And so that she could thenceforth accuse Mira of sponging the life and money out of Pete if, indeed, the answer was no more work.

Many mothers wonder this type of thing, but usually subconsciously, or at least quietly. Yes, it was annoying that she felt it was her business for even a second. But the thing that made Mira nearly bash him over the head with a wine bottle and cry with despair was the way Pete just passed his mother's question on to her. No consideration of whether it would offend her, or the fact that it had no worthwhile bearing on reality.

So why didn't his knowledge of and respect for his possible future wife trump his childish obedience to his mummy? Was he just afraid of telling Mum to eff off? Or had she simply expressed something he wondered about too? Mira was particularly bummed out because she thought they'd worked through his interfering mother issues months earlier. But was Freud right? Do some boys just love their mamas more than any other woman in the world and take her word as gospel?

WHAT THE GUYS THINK

ADAM L, 31, IN A COMMITTED RELATIONSHIP

You know Adam by now. His speciality is spotting the role women play in the needs and emotional make-up of guys, and his assessment is particularly perceptive here. In this case, the women in Pete's life are mother-figures, and that's what he needs them to be.

Remove or befriend

'He's got years of investment in Mum, so a nine-month relationship isn't going to beat that. What Mira has to do is either remove him from the mum or befriend the mum, and that means going over the top. The reason he sees his mother as the perfect woman is that his whole life she's done everything for him. No girlfriend can compete.'

One woman

'We see that the second Mira went away on holiday he went straight back to the other woman in his life. But if she sticks with him, she'll get him in the end, and he'll be so into her, it's untrue. This guy's no player. He needs a woman to smother him and if it's not Mira, it'll be another person.

'Mira needs to make sure that he doesn't develop a relationship (even just a friendship) with someone else while she's playing it cool and sulking at his mother-loving ways, because he then might start getting Mummy's feelings of attachment towards the other girl.'

So

'He'll always need at least one major mothering woman in his life. If Mira's prepared to mother him, it'll be fine.'

JAMES S, 26, IN AN ON-OFF RELATIONSHIP

James's mother depends on her son for her pride and happiness, so it's a two-way street. Well, that's not quite right. James doesn't depend on her in the same way, but she is the only major woman in his life and he treats her more like a queen than a mother. I'd doubt that it's coincidence that he only had his first proper relationship with another woman this year. Anyway, he knows exactly what role mothers can play for certain boys, and there's not a lot you, the girlfriend, can do. But there is a strategy to follow, which James elucidates.

Mother always wins

'Go straight to the source. Shouting or yelling at him will only make matters worse. In an adversarial situation, the mother will always win out, and he will ultimately resent being forced into having to choose between the two ladies in his life. Her solution is to do all she can to befriend the mother, and failing that, talk frankly and openly to her about plans for the future. That gets rid of any need for Pete to covertly play the go-between.'

JEROME S, 28, LIVES WITH HIS GIRLFRIEND

Jerome has got what I'd call a normal relationship with his mother. He respects her and loves her, but she's just his mum. Not his ruler.

Who's his mum? Miss Havisham?

'Is this a problem taken from 1953? What on earth is any modern-day 30-year-old on about if he honestly thinks his bride might willingly give up her job after marriage? For that alone he ought to be dumped. Then this business about girls not taking care of themselves these days . . . Who's his mum? Miss Havisham?'

Indeed. You have to feel bad that Mira even has to deal with her, aside from competing with her.

Mild case

'Despite the fact that Pete seems to have emerged from some timehole out of the Victorian era, this seems a relatively mild case. If Mira is truly keen on Pete, this is something she'll just have to put up with. The only consolation she can have is that someday she'll be in the position of the mother she so hates right now – doing exactly the same thing to her son's girlfriend. It all seems pretty bizarre and trivial to anyone outside the relationship, but can seem gutting and painful (especially to the girlfriend) at the time.'

Better she's alive

'And no man's ever going to tell his mother to butt out. The only one who ever did was Norman Bates . . . and look what the remorse did to him. Better to have mother alive and annoying than spreading a reign of terror as a figment of your boyfriend's schizophrenic imagination.'

That's it: mother rules, dead or alive.

BOTTOM LINE

Live with it, since there's no direct remedy. When a boy's hooked on his mother, you can't fight her. You can only become her. Or bide your time: she won't be around for ever. NB: mummy's boys are worth hanging on to, as they know how to need and love a woman.

What to do to get round Mum: As above. Charm. Smiles. No insults, no competing. Your prize is a guy who has the capability to love you with unusual goodness and devotion.

17

Why does he share you like you're a box of biscuits?

THE SEAN FILES

If there's one rule we ladies live by, it's this: once a man's been touched by your friend, you steer clear. Even if it wasn't anything serious, unless you think he's the love of your life, you just steer clear. A friend certainly won't give you the thumbs up, all yours, if she's still involved with him, even on a casual basis. Even if she didn't much care, you would not likely angle for your friend's cast-offs or sloppy seconds in the first place.

Guys, it appears, take a different view. Apparently, in some situations, women are there to be traded around and, as an act of friendship, actually shared (like Twiglets). The following scenario sounded mad to me, and actually made my buddy, whom it involved, laugh (and gag). Was this normal in guy-world?

THE CASE

My sweet, preppie friend Kaitlin was seeing a guy named Sean, a pretty regular bloke, early twenties, an assistant PE teacher, who lived with a couple of other guys. They had been shagging and enjoying each other's company for a few weeks. But Kaitlin was soon to be heading to Dublin for a work placement, so their little dalliance had an in-built sell-by date. The idea was to enjoy it while they could.

One night, a friend of theirs had a party. Kaitlin was busy partying on when another of Sean's friends – Matt – came up to her, pushed her against the wall and tried to kiss her. Kaitlin had two feelings: one was revulsion as she wasn't the least attracted to Matt, and the second was confusion. Matt was Sean's friend. What the hell was he doing? She was also bemused at his confidence in assuming Kaitlin was attracted to him.

She pushed him off and decided not to tell Sean – drunken larks and all that.

The next day, a Sunday, the phone rang, and Kaitlin's thrill of anticipation told her Sean was calling – perhaps for a date or for some midday sex. Either was exciting.

But no. It was Matt. He wanted to know what she was up to and, more specifically, if he could come round that afternoon. Kaitlin replied that she'd really rather he didn't. He persisted; what was she up to? Trying to put him off, she said she was going to a café near her flat to read. 'I'm coming too,' he said.

Believing she had made herself clear the night before and that he had acted out of a moment of drunken disloyalty, Kaitlin could only assume he was either trying to make amends or wanted to be friends, and didn't have the energy to resist.

He turned up, true to his word, and foisted himself on her with his dull chat, but didn't try anything. Until they went for a Mr Whippy, that is. Sitting on a bench, eating said Whippy, Kaitlin was rather taken by surprise when Matt launched in with his tongue. 'What are you doing?' she yelled. 'Aren't you aware I'm seeing Sean? And I'm not interested anyway! Why would you do this to your friend?' Kaitlin then threatened to tell Sean what Matt was up to.

She had no need. Matt took this opportunity to tell her that he'd run it by Sean, and Sean had said he could go for it. Share in the fun. Why not? Kaitlin was going away soon anyway.

Shocked and bemused, and also a little amused, Kaitlin told Matt she was leaving now, bye-bye, catch you later and have a good life.

Meanwhile, Sean was getting ready for a party of his own that night. He rang Kaitlin a few hours after she and Matt had parted company, as though nothing unusual had happened. He wanted to make sure she knew how to get there and was looking forward to seeing her.

Kaitlin stopped him right there. Before he doled out directions to his party, she needed to run a disturbing situation past him. Then she told him the whole Matt episode, finishing with the question, 'Did you really say it was OK for him to go for me?'

Sean mumbled and grumbled but couldn't deny it and didn't apologize. Basically, as it became clear, he hadn't seen it as an issue. Kaitlin told him he could save his directions: she wouldn't be coming along that night.

Maybe it would all have been cool if Kaitlin had fancied Matt and Sean had been upfront about their little arrangement. But to be barefacedly shared, coupled with the presumptuousness of Matt, who wouldn't take Kaitlin's rejection seriously, boggled her mind. Is this how a lot of guys regard the girls they're seeing? As if they can be passed around like a bottle of beer or a joint? Did Sean have chronic issues with respect, or was he just very generous?

WHAT THE GUYS THINK

TIM R, 28, SINGLE

Tim is a gent. Let's just say a guy like him wouldn't pass his woman around. Not only that, he's horrified at the very idea. He refuses to say it's a guy thing. Instead he looks to Sean's background to explain his odd behaviour.

Boarding school and gangsta rap

'I'd be interested to know the background of these two guys. I presume that neither of them has a sister, that both have a strained relationship with their mother and that they were raised predominantly in same-sex institutions. This is the sort of background that could lead to someone almost literally "objectifying" women in the way these two do. If I were older and grumpier I'd blame it on rock 'n' roll and gangsta rap for promoting the idea that you can just pass around groupies and "hoes". But, since I'm still young enough not to buy any of that twaddle, I'll call this as I see it: they're just scum. Avoid.'

ALEX S, 33, SINGLE

Alex is a slut. He has done everything, millions of times, with a lot of women. He's up for fun and games, but he can also get very possessive. Apparently, when you have no strong feelings for a girl, sharing her with your mates can be an act of mildly amusing fun. It's definitely not an act of love – for anyone.

Who cares really

'I could never share a girl I was serious about. The thought of having a beautiful little girlfriend and your mate looking over saying "been there!" makes me want to puke. As for all the other girls, who cares really? Generally, if you don't care too much about the girl and can't see a future for the two of you, then why should you care if your mate takes a liking to her and wants to sleep with her? If all you are looking for (and most guys are) is a dalliance with some hot little cute thing, then the fact your mate has slept – or is sleeping – with her probably doesn't bother most guys.'

Alex is a fairly typical guy, I'd say. A horny one, yes, but quite typical. When he says most guys are just looking for a dalliance with 'some hot little cute thing', it makes me cringe and pray to God it's not the reason some guys have let me drop mysteriously and quickly, i.e. that I wasn't little, cute or hot enough.

So

If he doesn't care about you, then he couldn't care less who else 'enjoys' you because he sees you as disposable. Literally a thing. If, however, he's more serious about you and wants a relationship, he sees you as quite the opposite: all his. Anybody else touching you would be a gross, puke-inducing insult and assault and theft of his property. Worse still, you become horribly tarnished beyond repair if 'shared around'.

BOTTOM LINE

If a guy is laid-back about who you sleep with, be it other people in general or his mates, he sees you as an object and a one-off. If he sees you as even a tiny bit more than that, he'd go mental at the prospect of sharing you, especially with a friend. You can hand him around too if you're so inclined – and this does, according to Alex, happen.

What to do if you like him: Tell yourself you're mad.

18

Why does he choose someone inferior when you're perfect for him?

THE SAM FILES

I'll bet good money that you have at least a couple of friends who are beautiful, intelligent, lovely all-round winners any guy would be lucky to have. And yet they're single. (This could even be you. God knows it's been me. No false modesty here, thank you very much.) You've sat by while your friend has been toyed with by a guy who ultimately isn't up for it, but she takes it because she's convinced they'd be amazing together and she fancies the pants off him. At the end of it, she is confused and heartbroken, and wondering why he failed to appreciate her. To add insult to injury, she finds out a few months later that he wasn't averse to getting into a relationship, despite what he'd said to her (hello, excuse), because he's now dating a 21-year-old bimbo with half your mate's (or your) spirit, sensitivity and smarts. Your friend was right for him, but he went for the bimbo. I've always wondered why guys make that choice – the lesser girl over the greater. Here's a perfect example of that infuriating phenomenon. Everything was in place – the sex, the chemistry, the shared interests – and yet . . .

THE CASE

My friend Louise is still scratching her head (and banging it against the table) about this one. She was so sure Sam was going to be someone special in her life, and, she thought, so did he. Her confusion when he put their amazing times aside in favour of a younger, dumber girl continues to this day.

Both music industry coolsters, they met at a big party in east London. She immediately saw a resemblance to her ex: the same dark curly hair and creative, broody air. They were hitting it off when a friend came and dragged Louise away. When they bumped into each other again later, Sam was on his way out, and they both said how nice it was to meet, and exchanged numbers.

She stayed and got drunk. Later that night, Louise sent a playful text to Sam saying how great it was to meet him, and made a joke about something they'd talked about. He replied immediately with 'great to meet you too', etc. They exchanged bantering texts for two days, and finally they arranged to meet. When they did it was electric. They laughed non-stop, turned out to know lots of the same people and were just generally having a whale of a time.

All of a sudden it was closing time. Both agreed it felt weirdly early, so they decided to go back to Louise's for a bottle of wine. Back at Louise's, they were both talking really fast, trying to get the words out all the quicker to get to know each other.

They were sitting on her bed sipping wine when he kissed her gently and tenderly.

And then he pulled away and uttered those stomach-churning words, 'There's something I have to tell you. I'm actually sort of seeing someone.' Louise felt a dull thud inside. Sam went on to say that it was 'really casual', that he wasn't 'that into her', that she was 'much younger' and that it 'wasn't a big deal'. He confessed he didn't even know why he was pursuing it. The girl, named Daisy, was a student.

She was 23, while he was 33. He said he felt stupid since he didn't know why he was seeing her.

They had sex and Louise and Sam went to sleep on the understanding that Sam was going to dump Daisy asap – after all, he and Louise had no ordinary connection and it seemed Sam recognized this fact.

He walked her to work the next day and, after dropping her off, texted her about his passion for her. But then she didn't hear from him. Assuming he was busy breaking up with Daisy, she left him alone. A few days later he asked if she was free for lunch the next day. On one hand she buzzed with the excitement of seeing him, but on the other, lunch is hardly 'I want to shag the life out of you and then marry you.'

As they walked up the road to lunch, he took her hand. They chatted away as before, and had a beautiful time. Sam snogged her before she went up to the office and said, 'See you next week sometime.'

No mention had been made of Daisy. Another week passed with bantering and so forth, but he didn't say anything about the key issue. Then, just as she was going mad with impatience, she saw him at an event that night thrown by mutual friends. In the pub after, he took her hand and kissed her in front of all these people they knew, and began introducing her to his friends. He must have broken up with Daisy, figured Louise. This was big stuff.

So, as everyone was leaving, she invited Sam home. Once they were back at hers, he confessed he hadn't done the deed yet, coming out with the old chestnut that it was harder than he thought. It was Daisy's final term on her course and she was relying on him for support – actually, she was much more into him than he had assumed. He'd do it, but it was going to take longer than he thought.

Louise felt sick, while Sam said he felt out of his depth with the two-timing and was wracked with guilt. In the past he'd gone from one serious relationship to the next, and this was the first time he'd ever just dated someone casually, let alone two people at once. She understood his point, but wished he'd spare her the violins.

The following morning Louise decided not to see him again until he broke up with Daisy. A week went by and she heard nothing. She was going to give up when a book he knew she'd really like arrived in the post. Surely his heart was all about awesome Louise, not insignificant Daisy.

But no. Another week passed and still nothing. Louise called him in a drunken rage, and when Sam confessed he still hadn't done the deed, Louise plucked up her courage and told him that she wasn't prepared to wait around for him any longer and that it was game over.

A few weeks went by and Sam called Louise to ask if they could meet. Convinced that he would never have called her if he hadn't split with Daisy, she literally ran to the pub. They were on the verge of going home together when Sam confessed that while he had split up with Daisy a few weeks back, almost immediately after Louise called time on their affair, he'd sort of got himself involved with her again. Louise ran out of the pub and that was the last she saw of him.

Until the other month, when she bumped into him at a club in London where his band was performing. Who was there at his side in the role of dutiful girlfriend but Daisy, one and a half years later. Why? Why had he stayed with the girl he said he didn't care about, who he was with just because she was easy company and looked up to him? Fair enough if she was the only girl on offer, but why did Sam toy with a soulmate figure, promise to ditch the temporary piece of fluff and then choose the fluff for a committed, long-term relationship? Pure and simple cowardice? Duplicity? Lack of feeling for Louise? Simply preferring the dumber, easier, younger option?

WHAT THE GUYS THINK

ADAM L, 31, IN A COMMITTED RELATIONSHIP

Adam is a pick-up artist, which means he's always looking out for strategy. He says that Sam, though he seemed innocent, had a strategy and that was to get the girl he saw as the best arm candy. And rather than genuinely worrying about choosing one over the other, he was having a whale of a time with both women. What a stud.

Straight-up Casanova

'He's a straight-up Casanova – a pick-up artist motivated by the validation of breaking hearts and being fancied only – newly formed. It's not surprising he's only dated a few women – he's come late to the pick-up game. He's in a band? Come on. He's learnt exactly what it takes to attract women. I'd say he's gone out of his way to bamboozle her. What should Louise have done? Ignored him. But she was invested; she fell in love with him because he reminded her of her ex. He doesn't have everything in common with her; he has stuff in common with every girl.'

Adam's cynicism may seem extreme – he chose his interests to pick up girls? But I have to say, those arty-farty guys, particularly the ones in bands, have always seemed mysteriously rubbish when it comes to offering anything concrete, but are very good at making you fall for them. (See the Alan Files in Chapter 8: the warning sign there was being 'into film'.)

'He's a typical player: he went for a kiss and *then* told her about the other girl, leaving him in control of both situations. He knew about the girl before he kissed her, then decided to tell Louise. You don't get *so* caught up in the moment that you forget your girlfriend.'

This is very true. Do not forget it. When you find yourself flummoxed and bummed out, as Louise was here, because a guy has made you think he likes you, but then told you something that shows he is not available, then you should definitely give a snort of laughter at his crass tricks and be on your way. You've sussed him out, and therefore his little game will no longer make you feel weak and out of control. That's the idea, anyway.

Cute little thing

'Now for the appeal of Daisy. He loves the fact that she's a cute little thing he can flaunt to his mates. He had no intention of breaking up with Daisy. Being able to flaunt the little piece of ass to his friends means more to Sam than a meaningful connection. This is to make up for not having it when he was younger.'

I'm afraid that this has come up many times: a lot of the guys who cause us torment and head scratching are motivated by murky motives that have little to do with a real connection and more to do with looking and feeling like THE MAN. (A decent guy who's not into you makes that clear asap, not after months of ridiculousness.) And here we have it. To a guy like Sam, who toys with you but ultimately lets you go, something else, in this case the need to flaunt little Daisy to his mates, wins hands down over the thing that Louise was after and saw within reach: a real connection.

Now, to where Louise went wrong. It was never going to happen – and here's why.

'Louise did a lot of initiating, but it was emotional. She fell in love the minute he looked like her ex. I bet she interpreted everything wrong. "Great to meet you" – that's not "I'd LOVE TO SEE YOU."

'Sam didn't cheat on Louise; he cheated on Daisy with Louise. Louise was the other woman.

'She wanted him to be the perfect man, so he made sure he was while he was with her – and you want someone to live up to expectations. Like all good conmen, he listened to her needs then satisfied them.'

So

Sam was playing Louise. He knew what he was doing as soon as Louise decided he was The One. The music, the literature: this was just Sam playing the pick-up artist. He wasn't ever going to leave Daisy. She was the one who made him the cool girl-getting guy, with her cute looks and arm-candy creds that he could show to his friends. Like all good conmen, he just adapted himself to Louise's overwrought expectations and made her believe he was meeting them. My word of warning would be that if a guy makes you confused, giving and taking away at the same time, he's doing a Sam, and it's all about making you want him. And very little else.

ELI D, 28, SINGLE

Now, this is a whole different perspective. Adam's is cynical and, I think we all know in our heart of hearts, probably quite true a lot of the time. But Eli's a bit of a dreamer. And there's a chance Sam was a dreamer too. Dreamers might deliberate dreamily over who they like more, whereas an alpha male, or a straightforward guy, will just know. This is what might have happened if Sam's like Eli. However, I'd say you're safer taking Adam's view. This one won't save you from pain and confusion – and pain and confusion are exactly what we want to avoid.

Dilemma

'I can understand Louise's side. She liked the guy, they were fun together, it seemed perfect to her. But, although he acted like a jerk, I can see how a nice guy can find himself in this situation. I reckon he really was in a dilemma, thinking about finishing the relationship with Daisy, having a great time with Louise – but then things change.'

More like good friendship

'I know a lot of guys who can never decide between women so we kinda keep two going at once. While with Louise, he really wanted Louise. But when he got back to Daisy he suddenly saw all the things that Louise didn't have.

'It also sounds as if what Sam had with Louise might have been more like a good friendship (apart from the sex), while what he had with Daisy seems more like what people call "falling in love".'

So

Sam wasn't a conman or pick-up artist, he was just your average confused guy who sort of might have wanted something with Louise but couldn't quite bring himself to leave Daisy. Both had attractive, girlfriend-material elements and therefore he just changed his mind depending on who he was with. In the end, he was more 'into' Daisy, but this didn't stop his natural interest in Louise. He would have been friends with Louise, after all, if they hadn't got into bed. ·

BOTTOM LINE

If you're a sceptic, Sam was just full of crap, meticulously employing classic Casanova pick-up strategies with his smooth moves and the leading on. But Louise was always going to project excessive feelings onto him, because of the association she made right at the beginning with her ex. It's possible he wasn't leading her on for kicks, but faced a genuine dilemma. Either way, although Daisy was a piece of fluff, she appealed as a romantic partner more than Louise. I've seen both and it's just not true that Daisy's hotter. But it wouldn't be the first time a guy has chosen a simpler, dumber girl so that he feels like the clever one who is always in control of everything. Sadly, whatever that amazing friend of yours has to offer, she's never going to be a match for the dumb, young option if that's the kind of guy (insecure, often self-billed as sensitive) she's fallen for.

In an ideal world, you'd recognize this behaviour as either just a strategy to play games and boost ego, or a gutless attempt to buy time. Then you would take a giant step back, preferably ignoring the guy entirely. You'd thereby be taking away an essential tool in his ego cabinet, and that's when he's more likely to deliver the goods you thought you wanted. Ask yourself if you really do want them.

What to do if you do want him: Make him need you by concealing the degree of your interest. Don't allow yourself to get carried away with late-night texts, angrily emotional phone calls and requirements that he come over NOW. Guys have said repeatedly that being too available is the surest way to put them off. And if he's enjoying the feeling of you wanting him, he probably also needs it to feel complete. Now's the time to withdraw, and send him running back.

Quick-fire questions 5

Do guys ever worry that they let The One slip by?

JUD T: 'Yes, but I think of it more along the lines of: "I'm
probably not going to do any better than that one." I don't
believe there is "The One" [singular] for anyone. Also, by
"slip by" I assume you mean they got away from you. I
always inflate/distort the feelings I had for the ones that
got away. I used to refer to "the one that may have gotten
away" as Melissa, the only girl I never cheated on. I
figured somehow the fact that I never felt the need to be
with anyone else while I was with her might have meant
something. Two months after we broke up, I thought she
was The One. We're friends now. I help her through her
relationship issues. Three years since we broke up and I
am so completely over it. I really believe if I could get over
that one, then there is no "one" person. Some just take
more time to get over than others.'

BILL N: 'Every time I meet a woman I like, I convince myself that she is The One. Over time I realize that this isn't the case, or in hindsight I might try to convince myself again that it is. But I know the idea of there being a "one" is misleading. There are lots of women who I find attractive and who I enjoy spending time with. Love can develop in those situations, and although the details of love may be different – i.e. I might love one woman for her taste in books, her sense of humour, the way she laughs, her arrogance, the idiosyncrasies of her beauty – the intensity of feeling can always reach similar levels.'

ANTHONY S: 'I did meet a wonderful girl who I loved so very much. She was beautiful, great fun to be with, a lovely person and ticked nearly all the boxes, but I was too young to handle it (24) and we split. A real shame as she haunted my dreams for a long time after. If I regret anything in life, it's probably not making more of an effort to make that work. Sadly now she is married and had a baby a few months ago, so, game over!'

Would you ever date your mate's ex-girlfriend?

What are the boundaries? This one's interesting. On one hand guys are territorial – maniacally so. On the other, once the jig is up they can be admirably businesslike about it. That is, even if they mind a bit inwardly, it doesn't seem like they fall out over it as often as women do.

BOB F: 'Maybe at school, but not now. It could happen I suppose, but many years later. I had an experience where an ex of mine went out with a colleague (who I knew well) and also had a date with an old friend of mine. That was awkward.'

MAOR E: 'Depends. If nothing's happening with them, and I clear it with my mate first, then I'd go for it. Why not? But probably only if it happened naturally. I wouldn't go out of my way to start something.'

TIM L: 'Yes, I would. I've never understood this idea that having been out with a friend makes someone a marked woman. There are some natural boundaries though. The amicability of the break-up has to be one factor. If it was done in good spirits, then I think all is fair. If she was the wounded party, then yes, I think that's acceptable too. If she broke his heart, then I think you've got the greatest cause for treading very sensitively, and possibly not doing it at all. But it's daft to have any hard and fast rules.'

What would you say if your mate dated or hooked up with an ex of yours?

MOE E: 'As long as I've had time to recover, then fair play. Nothing's going to happen again with her, so who am I to stand in the way of their happiness?'

TERRY B: 'Depends on which ex. But by and large I'd be fine with it. Good luck to them. Obviously I'd be a bit concerned that any negative stories would tarnish said friend's view of me, but you just have to trust in their judgement. I think most people are able to realize that there are many sides to people's personalities, that life is complicated, that certain personalities clash, etc., and so can compartmentalize their relationship and their friendship, so there's not too much spillover.'

Wow. How can they be so calm about it? I want to say that these are typical guy responses, but let us not forget about the mad, possessive, ego-driven, control-freakish jealousy that also characterizes the behaviour of a lot of men (mostly insecure ones, to be fair). Here's one answer that corresponds a little more with how women might feel in the same situation, though again, it's still not the rabid 'off-limits' response you might expect of what is often considered the male possessive breed.

JIM F: 'If it was a serious relationship, most guys would find it a bit complicated and weird to see their mate with their ex significant other. Basically, no guy would want to get into this situation. Your brain kind of cuts off sexual signals from your mate's ex, just like it does with your girlfriend's sister and your cousins – depending on the amount of alcohol in your blood of course. But if it happened, it's not the end of the world, like it is with girls. You don't dwell too much.'

Do you ever fancy your girlfriend's friends?

ALEK F: 'Of course. Why not? The question is what lengths you go to with respect to any desires. If we are honest with ourselves (not our partners) we quite often fancy other people, including their friends – and sometimes family, i.e. their sisters.'

ED P: 'Yes, absolutely. If she's attractive to you, then how can you not? It's not like her charms are instantly taken away merely because she hangs out with your girlfriend. Obviously you don't ever tell your girlfriend about this! I think what is interesting, though, is that the girls your girlfriend expects you to fancy don't tend to be the ones

you really do. I've found there are certain friends that
girlfriends forewarn you about – subtly, of course. There
are all these thinly veiled warnings about "Oh, she's so
beautiful" and "Guys just love her." These are all of course
coded ways of saying, "So you'd best not gawk at her
when we meet or you'll get a stiletto in the nuts." But then
you meet them and they are nothing all that special
anyway. It's usually the ones they don't see as competition
that actually flit under the radar and stir your interest . . .
or perhaps that's just me.'

Beware the plain Janes then, girlfriends!

GEORGE P: 'Yep. There's a special immunity with them – i.e.
they're safe because there's no way anything can happen
– which makes it all the more fun to flirt, which of course
leads to low-level fancying. Anyway, I can fancy loads of
women at the same time, but I wouldn't act on it.'

*How much do you care about pleasing your mother when you
choose a girlfriend?*

ALAN A: 'This question makes me laugh. I don't think
about anyone other than myself when I am looking for a
girlfriend. Maybe some people do, but my assumption,
and this has proven to be correct, is that my mother is
happy when I am happy.'

JOHN S: 'I'm not sure it really enters into it, but that's
probably because my lovely mother would be nice to
whoever I choose.'

Do you worry about meeting a girl's father or protective older brother/sister?

VICTOR L: 'No. I don't because I'm pretty confident. A lot of guys are a bit funny about it, but I've never been worried; in fact, I almost look forward to it – when they meet me they express shock. They expect me to be a wide boy or something, then they see I'm different. If you really like a girl, and you win over the people closest to her, then she'll stay with you because she always asks their opinion.'

BILLY O: 'Yes. I didn't till one girl's dad warned me. He said, "If you ever fuck her about, you're in trouble." Since then I've always been afraid to meet the dad. Never had a problem with the others.'

TIM B: 'I'd worry more about meeting the mother as she has the power to influence the girl more. Though meeting family in general is nerve-wracking because it means you're taking the relationship to another stage. But if you think this person could be an important part of your life you shouldn't back away from meeting them. As for worrying about meeting a brother or protective father, no way – we're not teenagers. I can handle it.'

How appealing do guys really find the idea of a threesome?

Like with so much that plugs into male fantasy, it's a bravado thing. The general idea is great for them, but the reality is inevitably not as great, either because it's too complicated managing various jealousies or because there's too much to concentrate on and that's daunting where penile performance is concerned.

PAUL L: 'Well, I've had a few. One was the worst thing ever. I had to concentrate so much I lost my boner. I tell you what though: guys who have never done it think about it. When you haven't, you might fancy it. I've never craved it though.'

MAX C: 'It sounds cool, but is more of an *FHM*-man-style boasting notch than anything else. I had a threesome, randomly, and it was utterly, utterly bizarre. The thing is, after you've had sex once you realize you only really fancy one of them.'

ANTHONY A: 'Now then, threesomes can be great. I have had two, MFF and MMF, and both were great fun. I think it depends though, as it's important that two of the people aren't in a relationship together because that's where the jealousy can set in. Some people enjoy the thought of watching their partner having sex with someone else. I don't, I couldn't stand the idea. So if it's two friends and they find someone else, or just some random hotty you meet in a bar, that's more like it.'

PART SIX

Objectification

'Objectification' may sound like a word plucked straight from a feminist lecture at uni, but I scratched my head and I couldn't think of anything that better sums up the issue of men seeing and treating women like objects. I'm not talking about crude guys who only see women as tits, bums and legs and nothing more. I'm talking about sophisticated guys, successful blokes, who have a deeply disturbing and very entrenched idea of women that, well, boggles the mind. In this day and age, it is bizarre but very true that major intelligence in women, especially when manifested in a successful career, is a big turn-off for a lot of guys. And nothing, it would seem from a good few of the men I spoke to, is worse than out and out ambition in a woman. Who wants to sleep with the gal who told you all about her drive to become partner at the law firm? Eech. I hardly need to point out that for women it's often the reverse when it comes to the men they find attractive.

As a woman who won't hide her intelligence, is fond of a bit of show-off wordplay, won't take crap from a guy who thinks he's all that and who loves a bit of an argument (though not on the first date), I've had my fair share of potential flings looking at me like I'm a slug or some equally unattractive creature. So it was with rage – this is 2010 – that I heard Antonia's story (the Michael Files, in Chapter 20). That a woman with everything to recommend her, from a good job to excellent manners, charm, wit and kindness, could be rejected because her intelligence and success were a turn-off made me uncontrollably cross.

But also curious. I don't think the guy was horrid to her, he was, I really do believe, being honest when he told her why he didn't see a sexual or romantic future. The question, then, was why he felt that way. What do men really think of clever, successful women as potential bed-partners? Well, the panel had some disheartening truths to say about that, both in the analysis of the Michael Files and in the Quick-fire section.

The Seb Files in Chapter 19 looks at the situation where a boyfriend is utterly unable or unwilling to turn off his 'other hot women' sensor. He has a long-term girlfriend, a smart and adoring woman, yet he – a successful, intelligent man – can't engage with the idea of respecting her by keeping himself from drooling at other women. Once again, such behaviour seems like straightforward arseholery. It looks like he just forgets his girlfriend is a person with feelings (not just arm candy) when he is around other attractive women. But, as you'll see, it's not quite as simple as that. And the bottom line for women in the position of Seb's girlfriend (her name is Katie) is to tell her man to sort his behaviour out and show some respect. This advice is not from me – it's from the guys. Which more than makes up for the Sebs of the world, I reckon. Ah, every cloud.

And finally, Greg. A man who puts dress size above all else, begging the question: how can a centimetre here or there be the deciding factor for a guy? I mean, wanting someone to look good is one thing. Ending it over dress size is another . . . and that's after trying to sleep with the lady in question on the first date. WTF?

19

Why does he talk about other women in front of you?

THE SEB FILES

There is an assumption when you're with someone that you find them hotter than everyone else in the world. OK, granted, Angelina Jolie's probably hotter than you, but your boyfriend shouldn't dwell on that. It's a simple matter of respect, right? As for other real-life women, it should be obvious that commenting on their hotness is not a nice thing to do. So why do guys do it? I'm not talking about your average leery idiot. I'm talking nice, socialized guys. Are they just not aware of what they're doing? Are they trying to keep you on your toes? Are they trying to be mean to you because they're insecure? Or are they just impolite, insensitive pervs?

THE CASE

Seb, a highly socially skilled history teacher in his late thirties, thinks nothing of commenting on the hotness of other women in front of his girlfriend, my waiflike friend Katie. Thing is, Seb is super-keen on Katie:

he is never to be seen with her without his tongue in her throat and he talks about her non-stop. She has recently moved in with him and they seem to have one of those symbiotic, do-everything-together-style relationships.

So I was a little taken aback recently when I found myself in their presence at a party. Seb was as charming as ever, but kept making dodgy eye contact with me when we were talking, looking over my head every two seconds and fidgeting. I could tell he was scoping out better social options, and indeed he quickly interrupted himself to say, 'Sorry, I'm just checking out that incredibly hot blonde girl over there on the step.' Poor Katie – who was right there – just shrugged apologetically. A pained look came over her face. Meanwhile, the drool was practically dribbling from his chin and he was barely focusing – and no reassuring pat or grin for Katie, either.

This was clearly a normal occurrence in their relationship, but not (for her) a pleasant one. The weird thing is that he seems like a good guy, Katie's a good girl, they have amazing chemistry and appear to be very attached. So why does he make those sorts of comments? Is it just thoughtlessness? Is he trying to make a point, such as proving some kind of freedom? Or is he just an all-out, shameless womanizer who can't help but ogle and objectify women?

WHAT THE GUYS THINK

KARL B, 33, IN A SERIOUS RELATIONSHIP

Karl is a total rock and always behaves in a gentlemanly way. In this case, he spies a nasty habit that's all about Seb's desire to prove to himself he's still a total studmuffin. The fact that he's getting on a bit – late thirties – has to play a role. Then there's the fact that it's a way to make Katie feel insecure and therefore to get her to cling.

I'm the man

'He's a womanizer, it's obvious. Womanizers are always looking for a big kick from other women – and they still want it when in a relationship. Is he saying it to get a reaction from her? No. It's just a habit. There could even be a bit of sexual excitement if he's standing there talking to you, with his girlfriend nearby, and he's talking about another girl. It's a power thing as well: "I have you, but I could have her too." It keeps her on edge, keeps her clinging.'

Again, ladies, the best way to judge whether a man is a good thing or not is to look at how you feel. If you feel like you're on edge, he's doing something wrong to make you feel that way.

Wants it both ways

'He's in a relationship now, but he misses being single; he wants it both ways. To have a need of that type and power is shitty but pretty common. Basically, he's under the impression that he can have everyone or he can just zip into action whenever he wants.'

So

His head's too big and he has got into bad habits stemming from his fondness for thinking he can have his cake and eat it. Oh, and he doesn't respect her.

JEREMY A, 40, ENGAGED

Now here's a different take on it. Jeremy points out that, bizarrely, there's a bright side to Seb's little habit. Not sure I know many girls who would be able to look on the bright side of this, however.

You can trust me

'It's a confidence thing and Katie should be ecstatic. Why? Because Seb is sending two messages here. The first, our relationship is so solid and I feel so comfortable with you that I can tell you when another girl is hot (as he or she would do with their friends). The second, you can trust me. And this is important. Katie needs to start worrying when Seb *stops* telling her how hot a woman is. He is an extrovert. He is sharing his internal monologue with his partner because he feels that both of them are secure enough to deal with that. If he stops, then his internal monologue has changed. He will no longer be ogling women in a (slightly politically incorrect) aesthetic way. He will be feeling guilty that he fancies them more than Katie and that perhaps he is feeling a little unsatisfied in the relationship.'

So

If your boyfriend is an extrovert, take comfort that he's revealing his inner monologue to you. It means he doesn't fancy them enough to keep it secret and therefore there is no threat. You can, if you're up to it, take the comments as a sign that your man is living out the dream of the fully secure relationship. Of course, if the result is that it makes you feel shitty, you'd better let him know you'd prefer a slightly less honest relationship.

ANTHONY A, 29, MAJOR WOMAN-HUNTER

Anthony never tires of the sight of a hot woman, so he's in a perfect position to sympathize with, or explain, Seb's behaviour.

Involuntary

'I have done this kind of thing before – gesticulated or produced some kind of reaction that lets the girl you are with know that you have noticed and are clearly paying attention to another girl. Sometimes you just don't know you're doing it. It's like seeing a girl with lovely blonde hair: my natural reaction is always a double take, involuntarily.'

(As for the power of the blonde, see the quick-fire question on page 276, on whether men really do prefer blondes.)

Testing

'But Seb sounds like a bit of a plum, and it's part testing Katie to see her reaction, and part arrogance. If you really care about a girl I don't think you make that mistake and insult her by praising other girls to her face. Maybe once, but not a second time. If it's not said for a reaction it just shows stupidity. I have learnt from relationships that trying to test each other with situations like this generally means a lose/lose situation.'

Lots of pretty girls out there

'I'm sure Katie is very pretty and lovely, but there are lots of pretty girls out there, and no doubt the chap hasn't slept with nearly enough of them to satisfy his needs.'

So

Katie should bring it up with him, but he's likely to keep doing it, because he isn't too into her and/or genuinely does want to screw other women. Sometimes the simplest explanation is the true one: he ogles other women because he does want to have sex with them. And as Anthony well knows, some guys are never satisfied. The bedpost has to be completely covered in notches before they can contemplate settling down – and even then there's a new bed, just waiting to be marked afresh.

BOTTOM LINE

Seb may be finding it hard to break old habits; he may be utterly unaware of what he's doing. The first step is for Katie to raise it with him. He'll have little excuse to keep going afterwards, and whether he does or not will be the only test needed of his respect and care for her. As it stands, respect – and possibly attachment – is thin on the ground.

Thing is, when you fancy a charming womanizer, you have to make your peace with it a bit. He's not Mr Good Husband material. But he's also a hell of a lot more fun, and that's why it's a toss-up between the good times and the dull ache of putting up with hurtful rubbish.

What to do if your man ogles other women in front of you: Ask him why he does this. When he's answered you can say, 'Well, pal, I don't like it.' Regardless of what he says, at least he's had to explain himself, and that will be good for him and you. It might wake him up to his ridiculous behaviour. Or, better yet, start drooling over other guys. A guy like Seb will not like it one bit if he feels your attention has strayed off his majesty for even a second. Lustful attention towards another man will drive him mad; then you can turn round and say, 'Now you know how it feels.' But if he's one of those guys whose lusty, out-there, womanizing character was what drew you to him in the first place, because he is wicked fun, you might have to just lie in the bed you've made. Or get out of it and find a new one. Old dogs can't always learn new tricks.

20

Why does he find your intelligence a turn-off?

THE MICHAEL FILES

Even if you were born as late as 1982, as I was, it's still likely you will have grown up with the idea that men are intimidated by smart women. Your mother may have told you this, possibly as a way of making you feel better when none of the boys at school fancied you. Or you may have picked it up yourself; it's a remarkably omnipresent idea, and not without basis in reality. Come on, who hasn't seen a perfectly intelligent man go gaga for a girl with a micromini fraction of his own (or your) intelligence, when something far more enticing (you) is on offer? The Sam Files, in Chapter 18, are about just that. The blonde bimbo is a figure universally despised by clever women and attractive to most men.

However, sit down and think about it. The blonde bimbo doesn't actually have much of a role in your life these days, does she? No: you're brainy and fabulous, as are your friends, and your brains hardly make you less attractive, at least in your eyes.

But then you are forced to see that, contrary to what you thought, some men are still, STILL, put off by women's smarts – and not embarrassed to admit it either. For a woman, a smart man is a bonus, as are smart female friends. But we're led to understand that intelligent and successful women make men feel unmanly and inferior. Can this really be the case? Isn't it more that men still struggle to appreciate these qualities in their feminine conquests and actually find them a turn-off? I think 'intimidation' is an excuse; for some reason, men still find cleverness unsexy and unfeminine. Because clever women who are also lovely, pretty and keen simply aren't scary. A grisly bear, or a maniac coming at your dick with a knife, is something to take fright at.

THE CASE

And yet my friend Antonia might as well have been Lorena Bobbitt for all Michael cared. She's an Oxford-educated lawyer, working at a top chambers in London. Michael was an advertising exec also at a top firm, and they met at a mutual lawyer friend's chambers' Christmas party – he happened to be best friends with the top dog there.

She was chatting to the mutual friend when Michael came over and began overtly focusing on her – it's hard not to, what with her sculpted Mediterranean looks and twinkly eyes. Antonia's wit and charm are both immediately apparent too; before you know it she's made you feel utterly relaxed and put you in stitches. Now, Michael's no sorry specimen either. He's got astonishing blue eyes, he's always smiling and giggling and his voice is lovely and deep (especially sexy for its Glaswegian accent). Anyway, the chemistry was immediately palpable between them and they were both raucously drunk. Two hours later they were snogging behind the Christmas tree.

He asked her out the next day, and took her for dinner later that week. Again, they clicked and had a lovely time together – and she fancied him loads. As happens over a dinner date, you begin to show your true colours because there's nothing to do but talk. Antonia's true colours are her Oxford-educated brains, overachievement at her commercial law firm and a totally charming character. She's laid-back but confident, assertive but highly sensitive to those around her and – like too many of us – just wants to be loved. Michael also seemed lovely, clever, confident and to have his professional star on the rise. After dinner they went for nightcaps at his, and got it on vigorously, but didn't have sex.

A few days passed before he asked her out again. This time he suggested a drink, rather than dinner. She, being very obliging (and keen) schlepped to his neck of the woods in east London, and they went for drinks at a hipster pub. She sniffed trouble: this date was a down-grade, and required little effort on his part. Still, the time flew and she fancied him madly; she hoped the whiff of offness was just her paranoia.

It wasn't – he barely kissed her when they parted ways. She asked what was up. At first he mumbled something about being tired. She coaxed him to be more honest. Then it came out: he'd been really attracted to her and enjoyed their time together, dinner had been fab, but he couldn't shake the feeling he was in over his head. Then, the day after that date, he'd been attacked by anxiety. She was too smart, too successful and the combination 'scared' him. She pointed out that he hadn't seemed at all scared by her (especially back at his, post-dinner), nor was she scary in the least, nor had she behaved in a scary way relationship-wise by pushing things forward or demanding instant commitment. Then he said it: what had actually happened was that he had stopped finding her sexy or attractive. He'd love to be her friend, but the more they'd talked and the more fully her awesome, brainy package deal had been revealed, the more his penis had wilted. He didn't say the last part, but she got it anyway.

Why did a smart and nice man find a smart and nice woman unat-tractive as soon as she revealed her intelligence and the extent of her success? How, when the woman in question is anything but unattractive, can something as positive as brains act as an ugly stick? This is 2010.

WHAT THE GUYS THINK

ROB G, 29, IN A SERIOUS RELATIONSHIP

Rob is one of those friendly, good-time guys who hangs out with 'the boys' and sees girls more like accessories – basically as girlfriends or shags or wives or mothers. He is a lawyer and, although bizarrely his girlfriend is also a clever lawyer, he understands the problem entirely.

Biology

'It's a real turn-off when a woman's into her career, always with her BlackBerry, very ambitious. Women should be intelligent, yes, but lovely and smelling of roses. It's just biology: it's hard-wired into us. It's also a control thing. How can a man be a man when his girlfriend is running a department at work? I'm afraid to say there's something of the caveman days left in us, when men were the breadwinners.'

This kind of talk makes me want to puke. And it's just cliché laziness – we could say that it's hardwired into us to give birth at 16. It's rubbish. And yet I wouldn't have included it (and I don't think Rob would have said it) if it didn't have a sadly recognizable truth to it, at least among a certain type of 'manly' man.

Bimbo turn-on

'A successful, all-round dynamite woman would be something you would have to accept rather than be happy with. Then there's sex. If you're with a girl who is an absolute bimbo, shagging her is a real turn-on because it's so much easier to objectify her and dominate her – and that's the ultimate turn-on. I always look at Bill Clinton and Hillary and I think, "How is he with her?" She's one of the most powerful women in America – I don't get how he can be into her.'

Oh dear. But there you have it. No wonder Michael couldn't get it up for Antonia – she didn't strike him as the ideal recipient of his doggy-style moves.

So

From a purely sexual, instinctive point of view, ambitious, successful women are less appealing to some men. For this sort of man, the desire to dominate and control in the bedroom is evidently important in the rest of the relationship too.

MARCO D, 26, PLAYS THE FIELD

Marco is another woman-chasing, good-looking 'I'm the man' type of guy. He's always dated pretty blondes. He also can't imagine anything less desirable than a successful girlfriend.

Intensely competitive

'I met a girl at a wedding quite recently. She's this Belarussian girl who went to Oxford and works at a top law firm, so the same profile as Antonia. I got her number but never called her. She did have a boyfriend, but I didn't think this would be a problem.'

Whoa there. It's a throwaway comment, but a revealing one. When a guy sets his sights, he honestly thinks he'll get what he wants regardless. Can you imagine disregarding a girlfriend so casually? It's blinding self-assurance. No wonder a clever girl, who might threaten that level of confidence, would be dangerous. And so the ego rears its head again.

'But when she was talking about her job she sounded so intensely competitive that I could just imagine everything turning into a bit of a competition, which is not what you really want in a domestic environment. It probably works out better when either person is successful in their own field but there is no direct overlap.'

Last thing you want is parallel

'Plus the whole notion of a girl being overly aggressive and competitive is not something necessarily that guys who are like that themselves look for. If you have to fight all the time at work to do well, the last thing you want is a parallel or a mirror of that when you get home. Intelligence is definitely something to be sought in a woman. But that stereotypically masculine competitive drive is not valued by men who embody and define *themselves* by this trait.'

So there you are: men have simply appropriated competitiveness as their kind of trait. It never crosses their minds it may also be a classic feminine trait, confined until modern times to other spheres like romantic rivalry and the house. Now, because we demonstrate it in the workplace, it's considered trespassing on something 'stereotypically male'. Ladies, if ever you start to think that the world is running along feminist lines at last, remember it's not quite there yet. Sorry for that rant, but I feel strongly that we should never give up ground, or bend to any idea that smacks of the sentiment 'women are meant to be sweet and smell of roses'. If your nature is to kick arse at work at all costs, do it and be proud.

So

Successful men are often afraid of meeting their match. They want refuge at home, and believe if their partners are as competitive and hard-working as them, said partners will fail to provide the domestic environment they want and need. They fear the competition, even if they're in different fields. So they'll take the waitress any day, but she can't be dumb either. They will have everything they want: the brainy, sweet, unsuccessful/unambitious sexpot all in one. It's what they do: they take (and get) what they want.

GEORGE M, 33, SINGLE

So, we've heard from the Michael types. Here's a refreshing perspective that will leave you with hope, and the knowledge that not all guys have Michael-style inner monologues. It's important to know this, so that when you find yourself wrong-footed by a Michael, you can feel safe in the knowledge that there are men out there who think like nice, decent, modern human beings. (For more on whether guys like an ambitious, successful woman, see the quick-fire question on page 210.)

Medieval

'Frankly, I think this is bizarre; I would never, ever find an intelligent woman a turn-off, particularly if, as in this case, she's attractive and funny with it. For a successful, intelligent, charming man, surely the ideal companion and lover is someone he can banter with, have fun with, engage in good conversation and feel proud to be around both physically and intellectually. Being intimidated by the prospect of that in a woman isn't just old-fashioned, it's medieval. Any man who thinks differently has serious self-confidence problems and a mixed-up view of the world.

'However, there is a flipside to everything I've just said, and I think maybe it comes down to ambition rather than intelligence. No one, man or woman, wants to feel like they'll play second fiddle to someone else's career, even on a first or second date. There are ways to talk about how much you like your job that don't make you seem like it's the only thing in your life. I'd give that advice to anyone, not just a woman, and particularly not *especially* a woman.

'Antonia should look for a guy who revels in her intelligence, rather than a loser who's put off by it. Let him stick to his idiots and imbeciles, as they'll be far more like-minded.'

So

Men like Michael can be avoided. Obviously since they come in attractive packages it's hard to avoid them entirely. But what you must remember, and what George (and other guys out there) strongly believe, is that intelligence, success and humour are a dynamite combination and anyone who fails to appreciate it – providing the career doesn't completely predominate – doesn't deserve it.

BOTTOM LINE

Lots of men, no matter how modern-seeming, still cling to this cave-man idea that they are the breadwinners and women should smell like roses and just look pretty (though cavewomen probably didn't smell that great). If a woman makes this sort of man feel other than the major breadwinner, or shows signs of doing so in the future, it has an immediate effect on the sexual attraction he feels. He'll imagine being judged or dominated in bed, when his big thing in the sack is to domi-nate a bimbo, to enjoy a pure object. Droooop.

Others are more concerned with meeting their match and having to face competition at home if their partners are successful and ambi-tious at work. They don't want that: they want a cosy refuge with a woman fresh from a day of dog-walking or charity fundraising or kindergarten teaching.

Finally, some men – and these are the ones to hold out for – think nothing of the competition, their egos or the breadwinning rules. For them, the more intelligent and successful the better. Chuck the first two types of men before they can chuck you.

What to do if you fancy a guy with Michael-esque tendencies: I don't think you should ever pretend to be someone you aren't, unless you are pretending to be someone stronger, better and more ambitious. But George made a point it's worth remembering at moments of doubt. If you sense that a guy might have issues with your success, just reduce the amount you talk about it. Focus on other sources of conversation while he gets to know you. Once he's hooked, you can let loose with your forty-minute rant about the sale of those assets to the Japanese bank you brokered for twenty-three hours straight.

21

Why does he act keen when he knows he isn't?

THE GREG FILES

Men, as they're forever telling us, are straightforward creatures who can't help but act in a straight-shooting kind of way. Don't fancy a woman? Not their type? End of story, no room for manoeuvre: it's not happening. I had dinner recently with a guy who told me, actually pounding the table for emphasis, that when a man isn't into a woman, he won't act like he is. So why would a man date a woman he knows from the beginning isn't his sort – either as a long-term partner or even just a short-term shag? Isn't that a really weird idea of fun?

I know that I've dated someone a few times without finding them attractive, in the hope that I will, or because I feel that I should give them a chance. But one thing I don't do in these circumstances, when there's a severe fancying bypass, is act all keen to shag them, or jump on them and snog their faces off at the first opportunity after a few drinks.

The other thing that's befuddling about the case I've outlined below is the fact that Greg seems so intent on sticking to a rule about body type regardless of other factors, like how well he gets on with Meg.

I can understand a rule such as 'cannot be a BNP supporter'. But a rule as empty as 'cannot be a size 14 or above'?

Greg, though, managed to combine both weirdnesses – the pointless dating and the dress-size rule – into one ill-managed shenanigan.

THE CASE

My friend Meg met Greg online (the rhyme was what got them talking). He is a divorced NHS consultant with three kids. In her words, he was 'OK-looking, nothing fantastic, just normal'. Anyway, it all began well. They started chatting on the *Guardian* Soulmates website, and hit it off really well. Within a few days they'd moved to texts, emails and phone calls, all of which were conducted with much enthusiasm and keenness, especially from him.

What with all the flurry of communication, Meg and Greg covered a lot of ground. One of the many subjects was their body types, with Meg describing herself as 5 foot 3, size 12 on top, 14 on bottom and with 36DD boobs. Now, only someone born yesterday – or in a different world – would fail to recognize those stats for anything other than those of a curvy figure. Meg was clearly no skinny girl; rather, a self-described 'handful'.

Anyway, they went for drinks and were having a super time when halfway through the evening he jumped across the table and began snogging Meg's face off. Couldn't get enough of her, or her curves. This full-on behaviour continued in the car park, where his curve-appreciation seemed even greater.

After a while, Greg invited Meg back with him. It was far too late – midnight and a Sunday to boot – so Meg politely declined. However, they arranged to meet the following Thursday.

Given the enthusiasm of the Sunday evening groping, it was odd that Meg heard nothing from Greg until the Tuesday. Something was up.

But she couldn't believe quite what that something turned out to be. She found out in the form of an email from Greg that arrived late on Tuesday, and which explained why he couldn't see her again. It was an odd mixture of blaming her for being too fat, while giving the ex-girlfriend excuse. It went on for over a page and was, to say the least, a little excessive.

He started by saying how excited he was both by Meg and by the idea of meeting her; he even stretched to calling her pretty, intelligent and fun. He went on to say that although he had known her 'dress size' all along, and had hoped that it wouldn't be a deciding factor, it just was. While he had specified 'fit and active' in his profile, he wished now he'd put 'thin' – more Kate Moss than Rubens. Try as he might, he just couldn't fancy a girl Meg's size. 'And since I will never be able to sustain sexual interest in anyone over a size 8, I don't think it'd be fair to sleep with you.'

Let us remember that it was Greg not Meg, gagging for the sex. For someone with a fancying issue, Greg sure didn't act like he was having problems in that department, what with all the jumping across the table and car-park groping.

Switching gear to another issue, almost as crucial as the fancying one, Greg wrote that a chance meeting with his beloved ex the night before had only reminded him how much he was still into her and not ready to move on. The point of this little story was to explain why he hadn't had time to email Meg the day before. He wanted to email rather than call so that he could present his thoughts better.

Now, a simple text saying he didn't think it was going to work although she was a lovely girl would have sufficed. The long email was inexplicable; did Greg really feel the need to explain in minute detail how Meg's size wasn't going to work for him? And why the information about running into his ex? Did he think Meg was so hung up on him that anything short of a long email would disappoint?

But more to the point, why, if he knew that 'dress size' as he puts it is so important to him, did he bother meeting up with her in the first place and acting like a horny bastard when secretly he was recoiling inside? He was treating dress size as if it were a core value, homing in on only one part of the bigger picture. After all, I love guys with perfect teeth, and prefer men with washboard stomachs, but have I dated other sorts? I sure have.

What the hell was Greg playing at when he dated, then dumped Meg?

WHAT THE GUYS THINK

MAX F, 33, IN A RELATIONSHIP

Max met his current girlfriend after months on Match.com. He is not impressed by Greg.

The banter

'Well, where does one start with this textbook douchebag. Let's break my issues with "OK-looking, nothing fantastic, just normal" Greg down. One: the Banter. Who asks about "body types" anyway, and what happened to the charming euphemisms of the personal ads in local papers? I'm guessing all Greg gave was height and build, without feeling the need to offer up specifics. He makes it sound like he's looking for a new car, not a girlfriend. Dick.'

Ah, that sounds about right.

'Two: the Date. Why Greg feels the need to actually meet this seemingly lovely girl after self-diagnosing himself as shallow is beyond me. I'm guessing that despite being a consultant, a humiliating divorce/recent break-up has left him emasculated and in need of validation. In steps Meg, and he decides to meet her despite his preference for a "thin" girl, probably hoping to have some kind of vindictive, aggressive sex with her (he smacks of someone who thinks that larger ladies are an easy lay). When this didn't come off, poor old Greg still needed the reassurance, the validation, hence . . .

'Three: the Email. This guy is incredible. He goes out on one date, didn't get laid, and then gives her the it's-not-me-it's-you treatment. Judging from the complete lack of any kind of appealing/borderline human personality in this email, I'd say Meg got off easy. I think this is all about needing to think that him not wanting her is literally too much for poor old Meg to take, and hence the ridiculous overexplaining and inherent I'm-sorry-but-I'm-just-too-good-for-you attitude. What a prick.'

So

Greg is a nasty, silly man who thinks way too much of himself. He displays a disturbing lack of humanity and seems to try to shag Meg because he thinks she'll be an easy – but inferior – lay.

ROBERT F, 28, SOME-TIME INTERNET DATER

Robert presents a different perspective in his explanation of just what Greg meant with his banter, advances and rejection. I don't like it, but it's certainly got the ring of truth to it.

Firm body

'The thing you're forgetting is short-term sex drive. This can prompt a man to date a woman he knows from the beginning isn't his sort. As for the hard and fast rule about size, I can understand it. Why wouldn't this be important? You can argue from an evolutionary standpoint that fitter bodies are more fertile. But more importantly, they also reflect the lifestyle and, to a degree, character of the person you're considering dating. And, at a base level, a firm body feels and looks better.

'As for the banter online beforehand, it was all fishing, no more than that. To take it as keenness is totally misguided.'

Well, that's good to know. When a guy seems keen online, before you've met, it should only be taken as 'fishing', or sussing out the situation.

Internet dating is misleading

'He knew from her stats that she wasn't skinny, so why bother seeing her anyway? Good question. Still, internet dating is misleading and different people will sell themselves in different ways. That's why it's so important to meet people face to face. Been there, done it. One girl even said when we met, "You look like your photo." What did she expect? She didn't look as hot as her photos. It was a good job that we met quickly rather than investing a lot of time in email, text and other banter that would have gone nowhere.'

Sisters, we love banter. We can fall for it. I have, many times. But for a guy it can mean something different – sometimes it might just be an ego boost, whether he is interested in the woman or not, and, in this case, it was a useful step towards a one-night stand. But notice how Robert skirts the question of why Greg met up with Meg when he knew she wasn't skinny, and instead goes off on one about misleading profiles. Meg didn't mislead – hence the mystery of Greg's behaviour. But what Robert's getting to is that Greg was probably feeling desperate, and when a guy is feeling desperate he will do anything with anyone – in the (very) short term only, mind you.

'Groping her and asking for sex: given that he was already on the date, there was no reason not to have sex in the short term,' continues Robert. 'The question is always whether you would go back on another date to have sex. My advice to women is always to wait until the second or third date before going further, just in case. On the other hand, if the woman just wants sex then why not?

'Women wonder why a guy will talk about meeting then bail. The answer is that there is no cost in arranging to meet. It keeps women sweet while you can make up your mind.

'As for the long email, it is weird. He is an idiot. But maybe writing it down is therapy for him. Still, usually you don't send the letters and emails you draft to get something off your chest. The line about not being able to sustain it is proof he was just after a short-term shag. He treated "dress size as if it were a core value, homing in on only one part of the bigger picture"? It can be a core value.'

So

Greg did everything, from the gropes to the invite back to his, for his short-term sex drive. He was willing to break his rule about shape so that he could have sex. And thin, apparently, can be a core value. Eww.

BOTTOM LINE

Both guys agree that a short-sighted grab for sex explained Greg's actions. But Max sees it as an example of Greg's vindictive sexual attitude towards women, whereas Robert sees it as natural. Both agree the email shows that Greg is an egotistical weirdo. And yes, some guys can be absolutely rigid about the thin issue. If you meet a guy online who expresses that as a preference, don't count on him changing his mind once he meets the wonderful you. Chances are, he'll stick to it.

What to do if you find yourself in this situation: Run for the hills – or for the other guys online – before you start to doubt yourself. Also, it might be an idea just to steer clear of guys who are so limited in the body type they find attractive. It's kind of creepy. That goes for large or small.

Quick-fire questions 6

How important is it to you that your girlfriend is successful in her own right?

Bit of a mixed bag, this one. Nice guys say they want their girlfriend to be happy – but we know that some guys find success a turn-off. Here, Jud and Alex both have reservations about it.

JUD T: 'I actually thought I preferred dumb and untalented and therefore needy. Then recently I tried smarts. An intelligent woman with a career seems to make for a happier couple in my case. That said, I find that really beautiful women just seem "so smart, so interesting". Like they have a handicap that makes even a tinge of intelligence look like brilliance. However, a moderately attractive woman who is extremely funny, smart and successful can be great too.'

ALEX S: 'Success can as often as not be evidence of things to avoid: ruthlessness, cunning, a lack of perspective. This applies equally to males and females. Of course, a girl-friend who is successful is likely to be confident and happy, and those are qualities that make somebody easier to live with. But the field would also matter a lot. The success would have to be something I admired – not a successful lawyer, say.'

GUY P: 'It's important to me that my girlfriend is successful in her own right, mainly so she is happy. If she's success-ful, it means we're more likely to be happy and financially secure as a couple. Any man who feels threatened by their partner being successful is living in the dark ages.'

JAMES B: 'I don't think it's especially important to me for a girlfriend to be successful per se, but I do like girls who are fierce, and that normally sits alongside being driven. But for some people I know, a successful girlfriend, especially in an area close to theirs, would make them distinctly uneasy. Having said that, I'm an insanely jealous person anyway, so if a girlfriend was successful in some-thing I aspired to, I'm sure I'd find it difficult. Of course, I'd first have to get a girlfriend . . .'

Would you mind dating a woman who was stupid if she was really beautiful? And would you rather date a woman with a sense of humour or a beautiful face?

TIM V: 'Sure I'd date a stupid woman. I'm not sure how long it would last – being newly single, I suppose I'll find out. Anyway, women have different types of intelligence, such as emotional intelligence, which can offer its own joys. As for beauty v. humour, I think I'd be initially more attracted by the beauty, but then if she proved totally humourless – i.e. couldn't laugh at my jokes – I'd have to reconsider.'

DAVID B: 'What a horrible choice! Why can't I have both? OK, OK. Truth is that I have dated some beautiful women who I found fairly boring after the first course/night. But a "sense of humour" is a very female requirement, I think; men would put it slightly differently . . . a sense of warmth. Don't forget that to men many of the traits of femininity – big eyes, soft lips, curviness, delicacy – speak to them of happiness, of being adored and loved. It's probably something to do with our mothers, but classic beauty in that *Vogue* sense can be quite cold and distant, and probably draws other women more than men. We want that loved-up feeling which is best described in the demand: "Come naked; bring beer."'

Would you or have you ever said 'I love you' and not meant it, for example to get something you want, such as sex?

WILL C: 'No, I don't think so. I've said it misguidedly, think-ing I was in love when I probably wasn't, but never in order to get something. The problem, which I don't think is a male one, is that there's no convention for saying, "I feel passionate about you", which is probably what you mean during that first year of complete adoration and excitement. I don't think you know if you love someone until you confront real problems like illness, or the pros-pect of long-term absence, or that moment when you realize you would prefer to suffer something yourself if it would spare them having to go through it.'

JEREMY R: 'Never. I'm just not a very good liar. I'm more likely to say, "You're so lovely" or something, but never "I love you" unless it's involuntary and heartfelt. I must have a female brain. However, I'm pretty sure I have convinced myself that I was in love with someone in order to sleep with them.'

Do you have to think a woman is hot in order to want to date her?

Two opposing answers here, both representing a good number of the guys I put the question to. That said, I think even Adam's trying to say that he needs to find a woman physically sexy, though perhaps not typically hot.

VICTOR L: 'Yeah. I'm really superficial. She has to be hot, or dirty. She could look really horny, that would do it for me. That would get me out on a date. When you can tell exactly what she would be like in bed.'

ADAM R: 'Attraction comes in many flavours. I find a girl's brain far more important than bust size, and thus tend to find someone who has something to say far more appealing than a generic beauty-by-numbers who can't hold a conversation. That's a little one-dimensional though, as in reality of course being "hot" helps, but my idea of hot isn't necessarily what you'd see in *Vogue* or a lads' mag.'

How important is it to you that your mates think the woman you're dating is attractive?

WILL S: 'Quite important. Partly it's an ego thing; partly because I know I want all of my friends to be going out with people they find attractive and, assuming they want the same for me, it's important to me not to feel that I'm pitied. I think that's where it comes from.'

ANDREW P: 'My friends said that this was very important; I have a different spin. I assume that if I find a woman attractive then my friends will do so too. But what are your motives? Are you looking for a demonstration of status (look at what I dragged back to the cave), or something that satisfies some internal metric?'

Do you mind your girlfriend being close friends with other men?

BEN F: 'I do now. I recently dated a girl who was unfaithful and untrustworthy. She enjoyed flirting with other blokes in my face and loved the attention. So I may be extra sensitive.'

JIMMY A: 'Well, there are only two reasons that a girl's going to have more friends that are men than girls. One: she's one of those girls that like to stay friends with their exes; and two: she gets on a lot better with men. In both cases, something is amiss. So yes, I'd say it would strike a bum note with me.'

ANTHONY R: 'Not as long as it's not in an overbearing or obnoxious way. I try to keep my jealousy at bay. But it depends on the girl. I'm a bit suspect if the girl doesn't have many guy friends as a rule and then suddenly gets close with a guy. It's a combination of not trusting guys and a natural tinge of jealousy. But all in all I try to be pretty trusting of my significant other. To this date I haven't had any issues.'

How much has porn influenced your ideas of sex and women?

BARNEY F: 'I can't tell you how many things I have learnt from watching porn and seeing other dudes at work. I have learnt new games, new techniques and new unique positions. Has it influenced my ideas about sex? It has educated me, thus making me a better partner.'

ALAN P: 'I wonder if I'd have known how to have sex without it. And it probably has contributed to my idea of sex as being more than just the straightforward old-school missionary style of getting your rocks off. In a relationship you have to mix it up every now and again, and porn gives ideas for new and exciting sexual endeavours, as well as being a stimulant in itself. Sex can be fun and exciting and maybe porn has helped in shaping that opinion.'

Do you worry about other men ogling/appreciating/fancying your girlfriend? Does it make you angry?

JACK H: 'Yes and no. I like it when friends, including male friends, say that she's looking good or even sexy or whatever – they're friends, and however sincere their attraction, I don't feel threatened by it, I feel proud. But if it's a bunch of lairy blokes in public – say, on the night bus – then yes, it makes me angry, in the same way that it would if they were to insult her or humiliate her in any way, to do with her looks or not, and also because I'm sure that such remarks are almost always made in order to provoke and humiliate the boyfriend more than anything else, and I hate anyone who thinks it's OK to pick a fight for fun.'

MOSES B: 'No, I love the idea of my wife being ogled. I don't have any worries about her going anywhere else. It's a great feeling when other guys say, basically, what you've got there is really nice. It kind of brings you back to that initial attraction you felt. It's like with a car – you drive it to be appreciated, not to get it nicked.'

PART SEVEN
Ex Hang-ups

You know that Philip Larkin line about how your parents fuck you up? It would work just as well if you applied it to exes. Every relationship that ends is the failure of something that started out full of lust, love, promise and hope. It's grisly. What's worse is that not only are you not with the person any more, but you're both going to have to move on to others, and there's always the chance you'll be left mouldering in the wreckage of the dead relationship while they're happily absorbed in the next one. Hideous. No wonder the failures of relationships past can haunt you and make you unable to face the next one. As I said, exes: they really fuck you up.

But women are resilient – I would say more so than men. After a lot of crying, we get over it. We can talk our feelings into the ground with a supportive network of girlfriends. We survive. Usually we're game for moving on when we can and, for one reason or another, we're less likely to use 'ex issues' as an excuse or to be genuinely bothered by them when we meet new people.

And when we do move on (or just continue single and hopeful), nothing is more disheartening than meeting a guy who throws his own 'ex issues' out there. It's a massive 'Oh gawwwwwd' moment, because it sounds like he's making an excuse but it could be real. Whichever it is, you immediately feel like shit. When you like the guy, the sinking feeling is so potent and depressing that you are already numb with hopelessness by the time the inevitable next line arrives: 'So I need to take it slow' or maybe, 'So I can't do this.'

That's because it's not a quantifiable problem and it could mean anything. Most of us know it's an excuse, but sometimes we're so enamoured we fall right into the trap of letting him control the pace, treat us like crap and do whatever the hell he likes – all because he has 'ex issues', which can ebb and flow whenever and however he chooses. How can we ever assess his hot/cold, weird/normal behaviour accurately when we don't know her or how things were between them, or what the inside of his head looks like? We can't. We're stuck in a waiting game, feeling miserable, until the ex issues have gone away. But they never really do, do they? How ingenious. So I wanted to know, is any of it real or is it just an excuse?

In this section we have a guy for whom ex issues are all too real and a guy for whom they're almost compulsive – as well as a guy who uses them as a way of calling the shots. (Learn to spot dudes like him and you'll save yourself a lot of heartache down the line.)

On the surface, the stories of these three men are related by the common theme of ex hang-ups. But what's interesting, as the panel's feedback shows us, is that each story actually taps into different elements of the male psyche. Joe's behaviour is all about the destructive dominance of the male ego; Dan's is a product of emotional repression and Nathan – well, he's just a player. At least, that's what the guys said. These stories are not only for women who have been fed the ex excuse, but also for any woman who has been on the receiving end of her ex-boyfriend's crap.

The Quick-fire section at the end provides answers to those particularly niggling questions about guys and their former girlfriends. Yes, they do think about their exes when they're with you, and yes, they love, love, love break-up sex. See page 249 for more.

22

Why is he possessive long after he dumped you?

THE JOE FILES

I'm the first to admit to that violent stab of sick-inducing anger when a guy I've got some claim over appears to be about to snog the face off another girl, or have a 'friendly' meeting with his ex. So I guess you could say that I'm possessive. Who the hell isn't? Certainly guys are, if their girlfriend spends the whole night humouring pervs at the bar, or dancing with a hot bouncer, or seems on the verge of cheating all the time. In those circumstances, it's fair enough to get upset. (No insults though, please: I'd never get too serious with someone who had a yelling or other nasty streak, no matter how visible my bra on a night out with my ex.)

But back to me and pretty much every girl I know: the second we stop being with someone, we know that we have given up our right to get mad at our ex about who they're boning or scoping or marrying. Even if sometimes we do anyway.

But here's the thing. If we reject a guy because we don't fancy them enough, we would not care about who they were flirting with. We would not be possessive. We'd move on to a guy we did fancy enough. Game OVER.

So why does a guy care about what you do or who you're with when he's not that into you?

THE CASE

Take the supremely puzzling example of the on-off relationship between my friend Jessica and a hot architect named Joe. Why, after Joe repeatedly broke things off with Jessica, did he go as mental as the most jealous of boyfriends at the thought of her with other guys?

Jessica and Joe got together in the most exciting of ways and for a while there it all seemed a bed of roses. They were set up, and couldn't believe their luck. Jessica is a man magnet with an awesome figure (one of those enviably curvy girls with a perpetually tanned washboard stomach) and Joe has the body of a god – he is tall, sculpted and lean. He was broody and mysterious, yet gentlemanly and keen. Each date was more charged than the last, and the sex was brain-blowingly good.

In fact, the sex grew better by the date and the cuddles and nights together more intense and cosy. A few months in, he whisked her off to the country for a romantic weekend.

But then things started to go funny. He seemed to lose interest in sex, the very thing that had been most explosive between them. Whereas before he'd been like a puppy with a masterful owner, he was becoming fractious and touchy. As things in the bedroom deteriorated, he seemed to become resentful towards Jessica.

This behaviour continued despite gentle attempts by Jessica to find out what was up, and finally she was forced to end the relationship since he didn't seem able to pull the plug. Even then, he found it difficult to articulate what was wrong, but he admitted eventually that something was missing between them, and Jessica figured out that

that something was every girl's worst fear: he just didn't fancy her enough. She was devastated.

But they missed each other and remained in constant touch, inevitably getting back together – then breaking up, missing each other and getting back together again. One Saturday night, not long after round three began, she was out with friends in Camden, north London. Joe was out on a work booze-up. He called to say hi, but when he heard she was out, he turned psychotically rude and just hung up. Jessica rang him back and asked what was going on, but he fobbed her off, becoming aggressive about her being out at 2 a.m., the implication being that she was out on the pull or, rather, the shag. 'Are you breaking up with me?' she asked and he said, 'Well, yeah, you're a nice girl but it's not going to work. I don't want to talk about it.'

She was stunned and horrified by this conversation, but lo and behold, the next day he did such a good job of apologizing (he'd been drunk and didn't really think those things) that she was pacified and, glimpsing a chance for real progress in the relationship, stayed with him. Let's not forget she hopelessly desired him all the while, plus part of her wanted to fix him.

He was making an effort and being sweet, but things were still not right in the sack after the first few nights: he just didn't seem able to initiate anything. Odd, really, since his outbreaks of drunken awfulness were all about possessiveness and sexual jealousy, hardly the hang-ups of a man who doesn't fancy a girl.

Still, once again, the missing chemistry left him cold in bed and they parted ways. By now he fully admitted he didn't feel enough for her. But Joe wouldn't leave Jessica alone, couldn't move on and repeatedly said he couldn't bear the idea of her with other men.

This went on for months. They weren't together because he wasn't sufficiently attracted to her, but he admitted he felt all the potent sexual possessiveness of an enamoured boyfriend. Just the thought of her out wearing a low top and dancing with other guys drove him crazy.

He imagined she was always out with other blokes, and began accusing her of putting herself on a plate. It sounded insane.

To get him off her back and to remind him that he was the one who had the issue with her, not the other way round, she told him she had indeed hooked up with someone at a wedding the weekend before, some time after they'd broken up. Jessica had slept with him partly because the person she'd been sharing a bed with for the best part of a year hadn't wanted to sleep with her. Joe was deaf to this and all other points, aware only of the jealousy and anger roaring in his head.

She's done with him now, at last. But the mystery remains: why, when his whole issue was to do with chemistry and that 'missing' element, did he work himself up into a jealous rage? What business was it of his? And why did he keep getting back with her if he wasn't sufficiently sexually attracted to her? Why, in short, did he care who she was with when he wasn't into her enough to keep going out with her?

WHAT THE GUYS THINK

TOM L, 28, RECENTLY SINGLE

Tom explains that this business of male possessiveness without sexual craving apparently isn't as odd as Jessica and I thought. It strikes me as an exclusively male thing: I can't imagine ever divorcing lust from a general fascination with a person. If I'm feeling obsessive about someone, I'm not going to say no to sex. That applies to wholly inappropriate older men in positions of authority, for example. Or much younger men who are my little brother's age. And if the sex is great, I won't just go off them. Guys like Joe, it appears, are different. But anyway, to Tom and the idea that sex isn't always the ticket – that it can, as in the case of Joe, be anything but what the doctor ordered.

Sex can get in the way

'Sometimes it really is better for men and women to "just be friends". Sex can really be something that only gets in the way. It's odd, though, as you can have women friends who you are not attracted to, and yet feel you ought to be. Consequently, when they wind up with someone else, you do feel a twinge of jealousy; after all, you've got such a great relationship with them, and they're objectively beautiful . . . It really should be you with them! And it could be you, if only there wasn't the slight problem that you just don't fancy them. I've actually never been in the position where I did wind up sleeping with one of the people I feel this way about, but I imagine that if I did, it could result in something along the lines of the Joe Files.'

Again, quite male. If I have a great relationship with a perfect, totally hot guy who shows interest, there's no way in hell I'd turn my nose up at it. Don't fancy them enough? Not I. But that's just me.

Possible to see she's attractive without wanting to sleep with her

Ah, but it's not just about fancying. We're into the fear factor, and the ego. Poor Joe's been scarred by previous girlfriends and that's not helping his libido with Jessica.

'We start moving into the realm of the psychological here,' says Tom. 'It would seem that despite Joe's godlike physique he's had a rough time with women – his possessiveness implies he's probably been cheated on by at least three exes. The description of Jessica certainly suggests that she's the sort of woman whose mere appearance and demeanour could inspire fear of that happening again.'

This, says Tom, is related to his earlier point. 'It is possible for a man to not fancy a woman and yet recognize that she's conventionally attractive, and that he should want to sleep with her. When he either feels he could sleep with her, or, as here, *has* slept with her, then it adds whole new levels of complications. That's something unique to the male psyche, and is bound up with testosterone and pride.'

That would explain why women don't care about who a guy sleeps with if we don't fancy him, whether we've slept with him or not.

So

Men can feel they have a claim over women they don't fancy because of a sense of irrational pride, which women just don't have. Oh, and they might also not want to sleep with someone even though they know she is hot. In this case, Joe thinks he should want Jessica, and therefore should own Jessica, but he doesn't want to sleep with her. All this helps explain the confusing mess that was his behaviour.

Tom's been a little easy on Joe. He identified the ego issue beautifully, and the need to control Jessica beyond the question of his desire for her. But Joe's behaviour was somewhat more worrying than this. I say, if a guy has an ego and sense of control that are as delicate as Joe's, there's not much point in sticking around. Imagine his possessiveness when he actually desires you.

VICTOR L, 28, IN A SERIOUS RELATIONSHIP

Victor is my ex-flatmate's boyfriend, and he appears quite a lot in these pages because he's a relationship genius – though sometimes he can be a little old-fashioned (believing that women should always smell of roses and be lovely and that sort of thing). Still, he's thought about all this stuff more than most women, and he's honest. In this case he hammers home what Tom said: this is about control, not about feelings.

Obsessed with control

'Just because he's not so keen on her any more, it doesn't mean he's any less obsessed with how she feels about him,' Victor says. 'A man has a mind and an ego, and they usually work against each other. It's an outer-inner body thing: you can feel yourself screaming "What are you doing with that guy?" to a girl, while deep down you don't care that much. Your ego is going crazy because you feel you're losing control – but your heart is detached. If I broke up with a girlfriend, the thought of her going out and meeting other guys and being on the market would be as strong as if I wanted to marry her.

'Men are obsessed with control. That's why having sex doggy-style is so gratifying: there she is, in front of you, doing nothing, in your hands. It's a big turn-on.'

Thanks for that, Victor. To continue:

'I've done a version of what Joe's done, screamed at a girl, telling her how much I love her, when I don't. What happens is you can sense her frame of mind towards you is changing and it hurts and you panic. That's why most girls finish with a guy and not the other away round: women can let go, guys can't.'

Whoa. Now that's interesting. Some guys can't let women go because they can't *bear* to relinquish control. They are manically bound to us whether they like us or not. The need to possess is a whole world in itself. Poor men. But it explains a lot.

AMIT P, 33, SINGLE

Amit is cynical and awesomely clear-sighted. It's amazing how shrewdly he looks at his own gender's motivations. Once again, folks, it's all about the ego. Jessica the person doesn't even come into it; Jessica the hot woman who other guys covet does though, big time. And hooray, men are needy!

Profoundly needy

'This is an issue all tied up with male vanity and ego. Men are profoundly needy, not of cuddles and sweet nothings, but of female adulation. Although he can't reciprocate, Joe is dependent on doting girls to make him feel like a player, like a real man. And this need is all the more powerful with Jessica, since she's so obviously desirable in the eyes of other men. She's exactly the sort of girl every man should want clinging to his knees. He's basically using her for that reason alone, and his erratic anger is a sign that deep down, he knows it and feels guilty.'

Mmm. Guilt. That would explain the anger. Probably explains a lot of temper flare-ups, even those relating to different issues.

JACK P, 27, SINGLE AND SLEEPING AROUND

Jack suggests that Jessica may have had an issue too. Her propensity to take Joe back again and again was not only damaging to her, it had an aggravating effect on Joe.

I didn't go nuts

'I wouldn't say, from the sounds of it, that he was the only one with the problem,' says Jack. 'Whenever I've broken up with someone, even if, after a long-term thing, we've agreed to be friends, I basically lose contact. I don't feel any animosity to any of my exes. I do remember that, with my last ex, on one occasion we met up after about six months and I asked her if she'd started seeing someone. She said yes, and I did get a pang of something, but it wasn't jealousy so much as a certain sadness, because things ultimately hadn't worked out for us. But I didn't go nuts.

'So, with this, I'd have suggested she didn't keep going back to him to "fix" him. That's unlikely to happen and probably made the problem worse.'

So, Joe became even more paranoid about his prowess and manliness because he was being tended to so patiently. Jessica's admirable patience was taken as an attempt to fix something Joe worried he lacked. More emotional pressure, more erectile failure. What we need to learn from Joe is that it's our job to spot when the sex – or attempts to have it – is causing more harm than good.

Endless libido

'I think it's easy to understand why he acted like he did: it's drummed into men that they should have an endless libido, always be up for it and initiating it, and that every hot woman should instantly make you want sex. Even if women don't expect this, I think a lot of men subconsciously expect it of themselves. So, for Joe, here was this hot woman who he just didn't quite connect with and that made him go a little mental because he didn't understand why. It could have been for any reason, not just a physical one, but that's how it manifested itself. So, when he saw other men fancying her, or imagined it, he saw those other men as men without problems, or men without his problem, at least.

'She shouldn't think that the problem is just that there's no chemistry so why should he be bothered. That's a bit short-sighted. They clearly didn't fully connect in terms of chemistry and it ended up becoming a bedroom issue, which is a minefield of self-worth issues for guys and girls.'

Amen to that. So the failure to fancy was manifested in sexual impotence and this made Joe, then Jessica, feel shitty about . . . Joe. (Jessica felt pretty shitty about herself too, of course.)

BOTTOM LINE

Joe was suffering from the demands of an ego that wouldn't let Jessica go, regardless of his cold feelings. Then there was his inability to perform in the bedroom, which exaggerated his feelings of powerlessness and masculine ineptitude. Both factors contributed to his disproportionate interest in her dealings with other men. All this said, Joe showed nutcase tendencies and it is wise to let guys like him go and cool down elsewhere, find themselves or maybe go to India to meditate.

What to do if you still fancy him: Let him be and don't try to help him, as trying to fix him can backfire by making him extra aware of his failings. Remember that this guy is super-sensitive and paranoid.

Or, as Victor thinks, you may want to remain mysterious for longer. Men love the chase, and it's not for nothing that Joe was keener in the beginning before it was a done deal. But again, a sustainable, healthy relationship with a guy with Joe's issues isn't likely. If the worst comes to worst, get him drunk enough to lose his inhibitions and forget about his problems, but not so drunk he can't perform, and jump him. Who knows, maybe it will unblock some channels and allow him to loosen up.

23

Why can he never, ever, ever get over you?

THE DAN FILES

Women are the ones accused of getting attached at the drop of a hat (or the insertion of male genitalia). Once we're into a guy, we're hard to shake, and this is why we submit to far more disrespectful, crappy male behaviour than we should, for far longer. We get hooked.

However, once the cord is cut, and the tears cried, we usually get over it pretty fast. For example, my friend Natalie recently split with her live-in boyfriend of six years. Within a month of the break, she'd moved into a nice new place and begun sleeping with a lovely guy who adores her (though she thinks she might be up for playing the field). Her ex is still moping and leaving her angry, confused messages.

Men – the so-called rationalists – can be notoriously cold, no matter how long-standing or good-seeming the relationship is. But if anyone's going to get hung up and not be able to move on from an ex-partner, it would appear, bizarrely, to be the guy. Women will mourn for a while, even a year, but we will always get over it and move on eventually.

I know of several cases in which the guy hasn't moved on one jot years after a relationship comes to an end, and still regards the ex-girlfriend as the woman to whom no one else can compare. At least five former boyfriends of friends of mine haven't been able to form relationships after breaking up with them, and alternate between childish anger and tears whenever the girl offers the olive branch of friendship. It's all tantrums and drama with these grieving boys.

THE CASE

The story that sticks in my mind is that of Dan, a good-looking and sweet guy who went out with my friend Sally for five years. It's now nearly five years again since they split, but he's still so in love with her he's in a permanent love funk, and, though he has no problem pulling girls (as I said, he's hot), he won't let any of them stick. A big part of him is still grieving for his relationship with Sally; another seems to be holding out for her to come back to him.

After they split, Dan wasted no time in entering a depressed stupor. He actually moved country – partly for ideological reasons, but mainly because he had nothing to stay for. Sally, on the other hand, wasted no time in jumping into a series of relationships and mini-relationships. Dan receded quickly into the distant past – not because she is heartless, but because at the point they broke up, it was clear they were not right together.

Time passed, and their paths crossed every now and then. For the first two years, Dan would snub or avoid Sally. Then, they'd meet, and it would result in more heartache for the long-suffering Dan. He'd write abusive emails interchanged with emails professing his still-raw love. Sally left him well alone, assuming that time heals all wounds.

But the summer before last, when she was on holiday in New York, where he has been living since they split, they had an encounter that showed how far from over her he was. Since they have so much shared history, they have a lot of friends in common, and they ended up seeing each other a few times. He was actually seeing someone at the time, but dropped her the second Sally rocked up.

It was after he had seen her twice that Dan asked her out for a drink – as a date. But it was so out of whack with every signal Sally had sent, and every deep chat about where things stood between them, that she almost laughed. Instead, she looked at him with pity and gently explained – again – that they were not going to have any dates.

Still Dan wasn't deterred or, rather, couldn't accept the truth. They were at a mutual friend's birthday party, and Sally was getting closer and closer to hooking up with another guy, Jake, who she'd fancied for ages. She and Jake were in the kitchen, having the heart-to-heart that would result in a relationship, when suddenly Dan appeared. He'd been looking for Sally and when he saw her with Jake he flipped. He threw a bottle of wine to the ground, yelled obscenities at both Jake and Sally and stormed off in tears.

They didn't speak again until a mutual friend's wedding last summer. Since they'd last met, Sally had heard he'd seen a couple of people, and thought maybe – finally – he was over her. They had a heart-to-heart at the wedding and, guess what, he confessed he hadn't moved on at all, and it ended with tears on Dan's part.

What's going on with guys who haven't got over someone they broke up with years before, despite being attractive, clever and having loads of friends? Is it a commitment to masochism? Are they obsessed with an idealized version of the ex, and not facing up to the reality? Even if Sally was the most significant relationship Dan had ever had, why did he just assume that nobody could ever take her place? He's not 90 years old; he was 22 when they split. Is there a chance his refusal to get over Sally has become a crutch – a comfortable way of avoiding new things? Or are men just less adaptable than women?

WHAT THE GUYS THINK

VICTOR L, 28, IN A SERIOUS RELATIONSHIP

As I said in the previous chapter, Victor has thought about relationships as much as most women and quite possibly more. The scary thing is that he appears to have cracked almost every mystery between the genders going. In short, he's a total find. Anyway, my long-standing curiosity about this whole guys-not-getting-over-it thing was finally satisfied by him. Miraculous.

No chocolate and Sauv Blanc

'When a girl finishes with a guy, she'll get together with her friends for Sauv Blanc and chocolate and be really upset. She will cry her eyes out, speak to all her closest friends and purge the guy from her system. By contrast, a guy will stand there with his mates and say, "Yeah, I'm pretty upset about it but it'll be OK."'

He'll then go and shag around to prove that it'll be OK. But it's not. If only guys had Sauv-Blanc-and-chocolate binge parties.

And what follows from this shagging-in-place-of-stuffing-yourself-with-your-mates? You guessed it. Stifled emotions. And that leads to trouble.

The woman in your head

'This emotional repression that guys are forced into by social norms causes longer-term problems,' declares Victor. 'He never fully gets over her because he never cries. In keeping quiet, your mind starts to play tricks on you, making the girl into the ideal woman. My first girlfriend, Roxanne – well, I just could not get over her. For five years I was shit-scared to see her and nothing compared to her. I had created this woman in my head that was not actually her. The woman in my head when we finished was far better than the woman I went out with. Thoughts of these women become like scabs, which you pick.'

I know the feeling from Facebook-stalking of ex-boyfriends or ex-flames. And, of course, from scabs.

Lost your soulmate and therapist

'There's another reason men can't get over close girlfriends. We are so unused to talking about anything deep or real – we don't talk about that stuff with guys. With a girl you reveal your innermost thoughts and feelings; it's like she's a therapist. A guy will open up to a girl like to nobody else, whereas the woman shares her depth with all her friends. When it's finished, it's easy to feel like you've lost the only person in the world you can reveal your fears and weaknesses to.'

How true that we share our depth with lots of people. Some of us actually share *more* of it with other people. I for one have always shared my deepest and darkest emotions with my friends more easily than with a man.

Women and their portable love

'Women have this amazing portability with their love. If she's been in love once she can almost transfer the feeling to another man. But a guy can't; he has to build it all up again from scratch. Women can rebound; men can't. Men can shag after a break-up, but not rebound into a relationship.'

So

No wonder guys can't move on. They have no outlet to express their feelings, so they just fester. And they feel like they've lost their special therapist too. Shagging around is only an unsatisfactory stopgap. It has nothing to do with readiness or desire to move on. You start to feel for the poor things, you really do. Not to be able to cry to your heart's content, and spill every last bean with your friends after a break-up, must be torture.

PAUL W, 32, 'IT'S COMPLICATED'

Paul is a good, honest guy who also happens to be attractive and endowed with a superbly chiselled jaw. In other words, he has a lot of choice when it comes to women, and yet . . .

Eleven years on

'This question made we wince, because I am exactly one of those men who find it difficult to move on from past relationships. I am still in contact with a woman I fell in love with at university, about eleven years ago. She lives in America but we email regularly. She is coming to the UK in a few months, and of course I assume that this time we will be able to work things out. The circumstances of the split were unpleasant: she met someone else she preferred. But I can't wholly blame her for that because at the time I was something of a drunken monster. So why does the desire to be with her persist?'

Paul uses his personal experience to explain something very interesting. Bear with him.

Sexual point to be proved

'I didn't sleep with her. At the time she was only the second woman I had the opportunity to sleep with, and due to a combination of nerves, regular heavy drinking and antidepressants I couldn't rise to the occasion (on several occasions). So there is a sexual point to be proved, which, however vulgar, is pretty fundamental to my sense of self-esteem as a man and what I want her to think of me.'

Ladies. We cannot underestimate the importance of sexual performance to a man. It does not just affect his self-worth. In many cases it *is* his self-worth. Paul is a mild-mannered gent. Even he felt that he couldn't let the sex issue go until he'd been able to prove what a man he was. There we are going along without a clue that our ex is being driven mad because he thinks there's still a sexual point to be proven. We're too busy shagging the next one (ideally).

Take back what was taken

Many men believe they own their girlfriends, regarding any man who succeeds them as having 'taken' them, à la jungle men. Raaar. Even the rational ones, who know this is not how they should see things, do this. Even Paul.

'She was the first woman I met who shared my passion for all things literary – having the same interests is intensely binding. But the clincher was that, because she went off with someone else, there's a part of me that wants to prove to her that she made a mistake, that I am the better man, and what an awful thing it was she did. It's a strong man who can resist the temptation to try to take back what was taken from him.

'Men do try to make possessions of their women. They don't like it if their women are "taken", however much they might deny it. A man retains a sense of arrogant proprietorship, and it baffles him when this doesn't manifest itself as it used to – i.e. in sharing a bed, having exclusive rights to her time, etc.'

See, I told you. Raar. But also a little bemusing. And amusing.

Learnt in the cradle

Don't forget Freud. We are also partly their mother-figures. And their mothers don't break up with them.

'Many men behave as Dan did – with anger or tears – because this is the most basic way they know to get a woman to love them, learnt in the cradle. Because most mothers of course love their sons no matter how badly they behave, they expect the same from other women they form loving relationships with.'

So

The idea of unfinished sexual business drives men mad. As does the idea that what was 'his' has now been 'taken'. This last one is the hardest to get over, and most men have an intense battle with their basic instincts to make their peace with it. The others just throw tantrums. The worst become stalkers.

BOTTOM LINE

There are numerous deeply convincing reasons why men can't move on in the way we can, which get to the heart of what it is to be male: repressing the emotions that need to be engaged with most; the struggle to stop seeing the ex as his property wrongly taken away; and dealing with the feeling that he's bared all to this woman, and now she's gone and there's nobody else. As time passes and moving on still eludes him, his mind naturally magnifies the glory of the woman and that only adds to the problem. It's a sad story and, frankly, makes me grateful to be a woman with the 'portable love'.

What to do when your ex won't let you go: The only thing for it is to wait, and, eventually, he will meet someone else. Hopefully. Also, know that he still finds the thought and topic of you deeply tricky and emotional, so don't torture him. Avoid him.

24

Why do feelings for his ex suddenly emerge after a few dates?

THE NATHAN FILES

If a guy's really hung up on his ex, he just can't move on. Guys are more likely to do this than girls, as we've just seen in the Dan Files. But what's the deal when he seems to be moving on, and everything is going well, but then all of a sudden he just can't let his ex issues go?

Maybe women are just more straightforward – I hardly ever think about my exes when I'm with a new guy. In fact, the new guy tends to be the best way to cure any lingering thoughts about the ex. But my God, the amount of times guys pull that ex out of the memory closet and lay her right smack-bang on your expectant lap is truly astonishing.

It's happened to me lots of times. But is it all just an excuse? I find that hard to believe – especially in situations like the following one. Then again . . .

THE CASE

I very nearly didn't go to the party. A late and physically taxing Friday night (booze and too much dancing) was not in its favour. But the promise of a mixed, international crowd (read: fit, keen men), the knowledge that it would make my man-seeking friend Natalie happy if I went, and the fact that the bar was two minutes' walk from my flat, meant I ended up going.

I didn't see much to tempt me, and was about to leave, when I saw Nathan. He was like a sunbeam of masculinity shining through the grubby gloom of the cellar. I barged up and took over in as polite a way as I could, and it wasn't long before we were snogging. He offered to give me a ride home. I declined because I didn't want to seem too easy and I had another friend to meet. He had my number, so I'd done all that was necessary at the time.

The next day he rang and asked me to a party – how keen is that? I didn't fancy it, but he wanted to see me that night anyway, so I invited him round.

He rocked up, just as fit as I remembered from the night before (though a lot shorter), and I'd barely got the kettle boiling before he was kissing me. Still, when I heard the kettle click off I pulled away, went to the kitchen and made tea. It would be too ridiculous if we didn't at least try to be civilized for a few minutes; plus, I'd enjoyed talking to him the night before.

So we did talk, and talk and talk. We were talking and laughing and enjoying it all so much (a trifle self-consciously on my part since we so obviously 'had a connection') that we almost forgot to fool around. 'I really enjoy talking to you,' Nathan said dreamily, looking into my eyes. Then he remembered about the fooling around and practically knocked me to the floor with a freakishly hardcore smooch. We stayed glued to each other for what seemed like hours, but it was a school night so I kicked him out around midnight. In the doorway I told him that I was going away on holiday for a week from that Tuesday. He told me to text when I got back.

I did, and we arranged to meet. We went for a quick drink at the bar in which we met – both of us needing some booze to loosen up after the break as well as to counter the high expectations created by the last meeting. A couple of large glasses of house vino did its work, and when we got back to my flat we went straight to the bedroom. Just as things were heating up, he cooled down. I asked him what was wrong. Then he came out with the story that every girl is waiting for when she meets someone who seems too good to be true. He was still completely raw from a break-up with a girl who'd left the country for good a few months earlier. He still had feelings for her but was also trying to move on. 'So what I'm trying to say is that I might need to take it slow,' he finished.

Now, as any girl will tell you, this sounded positive. The bad version would have been: nothing doing because of ex issues (code for 'I'm just not that keen'). I told him slow was fine with me and launched into my usual spiel about being anything but desperate to speed into something serious. With him thus calmed (or so I thought), we restarted where we left off: hot, hot, hot.

We spoke on the phone most nights that week, a trend started by him. I was super-busy but promised to see him that Saturday night after a day at the races. I was tired and desperate for bed when we finally met up. We went for another local drink (this local drink lark was starting to annoy me, as was the fact that I always had to suggest the venue) and somehow it wasn't quite as enjoyable as our previous time together. Naturally, this had to do with my tiredness and not feeling on form; he responded to it in the same way I did, by talking rubbish. We only lasted for one drink and a bowl of almonds before I said in all seriousness I was too tired to go on. He drove me back – it was a relief to leave the bar – and I offered him a cup of tea if he fancied coming up. But no: he too was tired and had to work the next day.

Despite these classic warning signs, we still snogged passionately before I headed up.

Life then intervened and I didn't have much time to dwell on the fact that I hadn't heard from Nathan after that last tired drink. What about all the taking-it-slow stuff and the loving-talking-to-me and the moving-on-from-the-ex? Had I really been binned because of one duff drink? It seemed weird, given the daily phone calls of the week before and the quite bizarrely good connection we'd had at first.

A couple of weeks later I suggested another drink; I was feeling needy and was prepared to accept whatever physical affection was on offer. I made sure I looked unarguably hot, and I felt playful and relaxed when we met. We immediately clicked as we'd done to begin with, and the flirting was intense. However, it didn't take long before he started talking about where things stood. He apologized for his long silence (never mind mine). The reason was that he was still too in love with his ex, after all. Only this time he wasn't prepared to take things slowly: he just wasn't prepared to take them on at all. End of story.

We parted with a carefree promise to be friends, and of course I've not seen him since.

What irked me was that something didn't add up. Given the ultimate bottom line about his aching heart, why had he snogged me in the first place, pursued me in such a straightforward way, unburdened himself about his ex so that I'd understand about taking things slowly and then continued to ring? Because as far as I could tell, nothing had changed in his situation with her between our first and our last meeting. She was still in Poland; they were still not together; he was still hoping to move on. Yet the difference between the guy who snogged me wetly in the pub and floored me and the guy who said he was too tired to come upstairs was all too clear. If I assume that he hadn't suddenly decided I was ugly, what had really happened? Did it take me to make him realize how in love he still was with Miss Far Away?

WHAT THE GUYS THINK

THOMAS M, 27, SINGLE

Thomas has been bruised by love and has delivered a lot of bruising – beautiful women he doesn't fancy have a habit of falling head over heels for him. He won't even shag these poor ladies, let alone give them a chance. Which means he knows what it's like to reject women; he's an old hand at it. In this case, his view is simple: I was a guinea pig and nothing more. Harsh.

Role-play

'Clearly, he wanted to role-play his past relationship, and try to work out in his own mind what he felt. You were inducted into a kind of emotional experiment, in which he simulated what a relationship might be like with someone else. It clearly took the encounter with you for him to realize how much emotionally and physically he was still hung up on her. Old attractions can be revived and burst back into life in an instant, and your being away corresponded to his wake-up call. But the important thing is that he wasn't taking you particularly seriously at any point, probably never really considering the possibility of taking things further. He had decided it was time he tried out dating other women – if for no other reason than vanity and to show he still had mojo – and you were the first one to come his way.'

So

I was his test-run. I showed him he was still hung up on the ex. The second I wasn't canoodling with him, or about to be, his feelings reverted to Madame Ex. I, Zoe, was never really a contender in my own right.

DARREN F, 31, IN A RELATIONSHIP

Tom thinks the ex was a genuine question mark for Nathan. Darren, a zippy, cool media-type, doesn't. Read on.

Full of shit

'This is pretty straightforward, and it has absolutely nothing to do with an aching heart or Miss Far Away. Nathan's a nice guy, right? Straight-forward, well heeled, an intellectual; the kind of guy who calls his mum every Sunday and certainly not a player, right? Wrong. Nathan's full of shit.

'At first I think you did everything right: you teased, flirted and didn't come on too strong. Leaving him frothing at the mouth on the first night was also a good move, as was kicking him out at twelve on the next date. But then it all goes a bit wrong. At this point, as you're think-ing, "Wow, I really like this guy, we've got so much in common and he even gets my esoteric jokes", good old Nathan's thinking, "She's quite cool, but I wonder how far her breasts sag out of the bra." Basically, you've got Nathan hooked in; all you've really got to do is reel him in.'

Muddied primary objective

'But then it all goes horribly wrong. Why? Because he gets to know you. Worse still, he probably quite likes you. You see, my guess is that Nathan was only ever really after one thing: to get laid. But, as a decent-ish guy, he has to clear it with his conscience first. Which gets progressively harder the more he gets to know you. As you dazzle him with your wit and verve, you muddy his primary objective. So, by the time you're thinking, "OK, I've waited just long enough before putting out so that he won't think I'm easy", nice guy Nathan's thinking, "Fuck, I've actually got to know her, and she's well into me. She's a great girl who doesn't deserve to be messed around. That said, I do want to bang her. But, shit, I don't want to date her. How do I let her down gently, and still get what I want?" So Nathan – the great, sweet guy that he is – decides to feed you a slow bullshit sandwich.'

Yep, sounds about right. We ladies often find it hard to resist the temptation of a bullshit sandwich, and boy do we pay.

'The line "I'm still a bit fucked up over my ex, and I just want to take it slow" translates to "Christ, I'm really up for some causal sex, but I don't in any way, shape or form want a relationship." In this one single line, Nathan's teeing up the end for whatever it was that you had. It's his get-out-of-jail-free card. He's leaving the back door unlocked, so when he decides to do a runner, his conscience is clear – and you can never say you weren't warned.'

Came on too strong

'But there's a bigger question: what put him off you in the first place? This is much, much harder to answer. My guess is – after playing it so cool at the beginning – you came on too strong towards the end. Some guys might say they like a woman who's not afraid to approach, take the lead, etc., but the truth is: we don't. It just terrifies us. Pushy girls feel too available – which means no chase, no challenge and no sense of achievement at the end.'

So many times I have told myself that this guy's too nice/cool and our connection is too great to worry about something like playing it cool when we're obviously getting along superbly. And you know what? Every time I've told myself that, and let myself behave naturally, the guy's gone weird. I've always said it was just bad luck, or that keenness wasn't the reason. Now it's spelled out, by a guy (and a nice, clever one at that). There is nothing worse than a girl that 'feels too available'. End of. (You'll see the answers to the quick-fire question 'What is the biggest thing a girl can do that scares you /turns you off?' on page 34 corroborate this.)

'Now, I know what you're thinking,' concludes Darren. 'Nathan wasn't that kind of guy. The sad truth is: he was. We all are. Even your best male friend – you know the one. That guy mate who you let sleep in your bed after a late night, the one who's far too gentle, tepid and intimidated by you to ever try it on. Even him. Don't believe me? Check his laptop.'

Girls, this is testament to the fact that no guy is too good for the chase. Every guy wants someone who plays hard to get, seems unavailable, all that stuff. It is ALWAYS, ALWAYS important to a guy, no matter how brainy, kindly or sophisticated he is. Darren's point about the laptop is that no guy is above dirty tricks for sex – be that game-playing, pretending to like a girl when he's only after sex, or just a laptop porn habit.

'So what can you learn? There's a little bit of Snoop Dogg in every guy, even the nice ones.'

So

Nathan looked, walked, talked and smelled nice. But he played dirty, setting up a nice little situation with the 'ex issues'. Having put that one out there, he could have the sex and the fun but never have to deliver more.

BOTTOM LINE

Sure, he liked me (what's not to like?), but was never fully into me. The mention of his ex meant he was playing a get-out-of-jail-free card, which means he wasn't serious about a relationship – in fact, he was utterly against one. When I became too available, he tipped from not wanting more to wanting nothing.

So, ladies, the second a guy so much as mentions his ex in a whiny, I-need-to-take-things-slow way, get a last shag or two in and be on your way. Even if he thinks he's really moving on and giving you a genuine whirl as a girlfriend, there's trouble ahead. It could be that he's just seeing how it feels, test-driving you as Someone Other Than My Ex. It's all about him, and we don't want that now, do we?

But the chances are he's not even planning on giving you a chance. Nah, he's going to use the get-out-jail-free card to play you like a fool, getting what he wants when it suits him and probably more besides from other girls. He's done it before and it works.

Don't let him play you, though: catch him out the second he cries 'ex' and get moving. There's a little bit of Snoop Dogg in every man? Well, there's a little bit of Foxy Brown in every woman.

What to do if you fancy him: Back it way, way down. He liked you to begin with; he finds you good company, you're sexy, whatever. Most of all, it's both easy and interesting because you're not his yet. So keep it that way. It may be that he gets tired of hanging on to his pathetic ex-issues excuse because it's getting in the way of what he really wants: you. Thing is, he'll only come to that conclusion if left alone, feeling unloved, for as long as it takes to show you *really* aren't bothered (even if you are).

As soon as he mentions the ex, it's a sign that he's not that into what you've got going on. He's playing a card that ensures he keeps you at arm's length. But if you hold him at your own arm's length, the dynamic will change.

This kind of guy loves and needs a chase. If you really want him, you'll have to give him one. My mistake was twofold: I showed him that I could see a relationship developing and was excited about it, and I let him play his ex-issues card. That is, I let him walk all over me, so he knew he could, which isn't hot. I should have had the courage to say. 'Honey, you can take your ex issues and your sorry ass and head home now. I don't have time for that.' Easier said than done, but you get the idea. That's hot.

Quick-fire questions 7

Do you stay in contact with your ex-girlfriends?

TIM A: 'Only insofar as I want to know what they're up to in
  broad strokes. For instance, I want to know about
  marriages, children, moves abroad and dramatic changes
  in the professional arena, but almost everything else feels
  like detail I don't need. You can never be completely light
  and breezy with someone whose heart you've broken, or
  vice versa.'

ALEX B: 'I don't think there's any excuse for staying in touch
  with an ex. If you've got respect for your current
  boyfriend/girlfriend you'll sacrifice that one friendship.'

JACK L: 'Yes and no. I've only had two exes in the last ten
  years – I was with one for seven years, the other seven
  months. I stay in touch with the seven-year one (a hideous
  break-up) because we were so close, but steer clear of the
  seven-month one because it was all just a bit awkward.'

How soon after one relationship ends do you consider it OK to get into another one – i.e. is there such a thing as a broken guy who has to be single for a bit?

KOBI N: 'Sure, guys need time alone. I need about three months between two serious relationships. Of course, sex is always an option in the meantime. Or even a solution in most cases.'

NEIL E: 'Entirely depends on who the girl in question is. You can be "not ready" through a parade of girls if they don't blow you away. Then suddenly, at the worst time, when you're definitely not meant to be ready, you can meet someone you'd risk any amount of emotional damage for.'

Do you secretly love, or even covet, break-up sex?

ANTHONY S: 'Break-up sex can be great depending on how the relationship ended. I have slept with a fair amount of exes after a split and the sex has been great, but that's because I didn't want them any more. But the last girl, I still loved her, and it was upsetting to be so intimate with someone you love and know deep down that they don't feel as strongly.'

KEITH R: 'Well, who doesn't love break-up sex? There are two types: the kind of sex that just has to happen (like me taking my sluttiest ex ever against a wall in an alleyway before she returned home to the man who's now her husband). The other kind of ex sex is hate sex, where you hate her so much you want to screw her in a (legally and un-psychotically) violent way. It feels so good right up until about, oh, .000000000000000001 seconds after you

come, at which point you feel like the worst, most trapped
person in the world.'

Well, ladies, now you know the worst when he doesn't want to cuddle
after break-up sex. If you still fancy him at all, you'd better be prepared
for some harsh treatment. Only the tough need apply, I say. He's not
going to melt.

Is the need to take things slowly ever something you consider, or is it always just an excuse?

The number of times I've been fed this one is countless. I've never been
able to figure out if it's true or if I was being fobbed off. Apparently it
can be both.

ANTHONY A: 'It doesn't have to be an excuse. I think if you
are serious it's sensible to take your time. I have rushed
into relationships and maybe it would have been better to
get to know the person first. That said, when you fancy
them you get that little love bug and can't help yourself –
you start acting like a child with a new toy. So I guess
when you really like someone you can't take it slowly,
even if it would be better.'

KOBI N: 'When I want to "take things slowly", I'm actually
saying, "you're getting much too needy and attached,
please give me some air", so it's not really an excuse, just
a nice way to put it, without hurting her feelings, I hope.'

That said, men are emotional creatures and may have been hurt in
the past, so don't necessarily write off the 'take it slow' vibe. *However*,
if he wants to take it slowly, and he likes you and wants to make it
work, he will tell you why honestly and it should ring true.

Do you ever think about your ex while you're in another relationship?

This one is a major hang-up for a lot of women I know, because it's impossible to get inside someone else's head and know what they're thinking. Who's to say if a boyfriend's mind is running over a memory of sex on the kitchen counter with an old girlfriend? There is also the fear of the nightmare scenario, which happens painfully often: the trusty getting-back-together-with-the-ex move.

NICK H: 'Yes, I've thought about some exes while with some present girlfriends, but not all the time out of dog-like basic rut-desire, but because some are my friends. I find it hard to stop caring about people I have been that intimate with, just because the deeds of the contract have changed. But if the question is, "Have I ever wanted to fuck someone that I'm not with, while I'm with someone else", then the answer is yes. That's a warm ache in the groin that has got nothing to do with fidelity – it's an urge.'

TOM A: 'Honestly? You can't care less about your ex at the beginning of a new relationship. Chances are you've thrown yourself into it to some degree in order to escape the past anyway and you're totally loved up. But as your current relationship goes on for a while, your mind can start to wander, particularly as it's a natural thing to idealize the past (and the past's women) when things aren't perfect with your current girl.'

The following question may sound similar, but hell, it's slightly different, and this is an important area that deserves to be thoroughly answered, so here goes . . .

Do you ever really get over your exes, or is there always a part of you that minds when they get together with someone else?

ROGER M: 'The short answer is no, not completely, although mostly. It seems to be the last girl you had a serious relationship with will be the one you think about and stalk on Facebook when you probably shouldn't [Hooray! They do it too!]. Girlfriends before that you actually remember quite fondly. But that said, you don't particularly want to know about their new boyfriends. There's a danger you'll end up being snared by all sorts of insecurities comparing yourself to him, so it's best just not to bother looking into it.'

MARK C: 'A part of you never gets over your ex. Because no matter how over her you are, or think you are, or whatever, you'll never be comfortable knowing some other man is doing the things and sharing the experiences with the same woman that you used to do it all with. That is a very difficult idea for a guy. So yes, you never like to see an ex all loved up.'

Why do you think men are considered bad at communicating?

ALAN B: 'Over the last decade, mainstream ideas about how men can and should behave have changed, and men are more and more encouraged to express their feelings – but still this is often framed within strict boundaries. For instance, while men are encouraged to have equal, open conversations with their partners, they are still not encouraged on a more everyday level to think about how they feel about their encounters, trials, moods and what-not. Much less to talk about this "trivia" with friends and family. We're poorly practised, simple as that.'

JULIAN M: 'Men are never encouraged to communicate, and rarely talk among themselves about relationships and emotions – personal issues. Male conversations revolve around work, sport and often involve talking about women as conquests as opposed to the development of relationships. Then there could be the role of genetic differences (men inherently hunters, women the centre of family), social etiquette or even cultural pressure.'

CARLOS C: 'Probably because they are bad at communicating. Discussing feelings or emotional issues is not something that is enjoyable or normally necessary. I think it's nice if a girl is communicative, but it's often hard for a guy to communicate, particularly when he doesn't know himself what he wants to communicate.'

PART EIGHT

Essential Quick-fire Questions on Sex, Choosing a Mate, Attraction and the Chase

The following questions and answers aren't attached to any of the preceding chapters in particular, but they are important. The list of 'all you ever wanted to know' type questions is endless, so I cherry-picked after asking lots of girls which things they'd always wondered about but had never quite got round to asking. I hope that in their different ways, the blokes here have shed some generous light on several niggling matters.

SEX

Now, I'd say this is fairly self-explanatory. Obviously, this is only the tip of the iceberg (so to speak); there couldn't be a broader heading than 'sex'. But these questions tackle some of the things I and many of my friends have come up against and wondered about countless times. Generally, the answers are reassuring: once they're in bed with you, guys are too busy trying to enjoy themselves, and make you enjoy yourself, to think about much else. A lot of girls worry about whether they can get away with sex on the first date. In general, if the chemistry's there, the answer to that one is yes.

How do you feel about a girl who hasn't slept with many people or hasn't got much experience in bed? Is inexperience unattractive?

By and large, men are more grateful for less rather than more experience, which came as a surprise to me. I'd forgotten how powerfully territorial they are.

MOSES B: 'No! I haven't slept with many people either, so we'd be in good company. But it can cause problems. I had a friend who found that his girlfriend was too quiet during sex, not confident enough to express herself, and he found it a real turn-off. In some cases you'd find someone more attractive if she hadn't slept with a lot of people, because she's not the town bicycle. But in other cases, you do feel, what's been going on here?'

IAIN H: 'Inexperience in itself isn't unattractive. Being rubbish in bed is. The two don't always go hand in hand. I think some people are naturally good in bed (or naturally bad). But I think that a lot of men would worry about sleeping with someone with very little sexual experience. Why have they had so little? There's also a fear that they might quickly attach more significance to the encounter, which could be off-putting.'

WILL L: 'It's too much experience that's unattractive, not too little. I don't want some wizened old trout who's been around the block a hundred times. Enthusiasm is more important than experience in my book, and it's nice to imagine you've actually done something special to get her into bed, rather than thinking she's not picky, everyone else has been there and you're "stirring their porridge".'

What's the worst thing a girl can do in bed?

JIM F: 'I do not want any fingers in my arse, thank you very much. I really don't.'

ALEX P: 'Just lie there and do nothing. There needs to be some interest from both a physical and psychological point of view.'

What's the maximum number of guys a girl can have slept with for you to feel comfortable?

VICTOR L: 'Ten is the absolute max. If it's more than that, just lie. I'm a chauvinist because I've slept with forty or fifty women. But women aren't born slags; it's not natural to them to sleep around and keep shagging. They do it for a range of other reasons: a quick fix, to feel loved, want of attention, want to make a point, tell stories, etc.'

As awful as this sounds, I have to say that in phases of multi-shagging with people that I don't feel much towards, I feel numb – i.e. I do it for those reasons above, not because my groins ache for a fifth shag in a week.

BOB K: 'Less than me, by a good amount. Fifteen?'

MARTIN B: 'No guy wants to know he's anything higher than the eleventh on the list. Honestly, I'd rather the girl lied if she's slept with more than ten guys. We just find it tricky to hear the truth in this case.'

Do you judge a girl who sleeps with you on the first date?

MARK C: 'Not at all. If you like someone, you like someone. If it's good, you'll sleep with them on the second, third and fourth date as well – and possibly for the rest of your life. The reason women get hung up about this is that a lot of men who sleep with them on the first date never get back in touch as they've already got what they wanted. Women then blame themselves. A more positive way of looking at it is that these men would have vanished after the fifth date as well, if that's how long she had held out. At least this way you get to find out early on if he's into you or not.

'Personally though, I think the fourth or fifth date is a good time to sleep with someone – it gives you a little bit of time to get to know them first. But you shouldn't stress if it happens earlier than this. Some of the best relationships start with a one-night stand and develop from there.'

DAN G: 'I do not judge a girl negatively if we have sex on a first date. Do you judge a man so if he does with you? Sex, despite what the *Nuts* readership will have you believe, is meaningful to some men and not always an end in itself. Anyway, first-date sex can be fantastic, unexpected, awkward, etc., and lead nowhere or to everything . . . why would anyone want to rule that out if they feel something?'

GEORGE M: 'No, I wouldn't necessarily think a girl was promiscuous because she slept with me on a first date. If it felt right, then why not? But there would probably be the creeping fear that starting with a bang means the relationship might fizzle out fast. I've always preferred to build up to sex incrementally. That's a lot more fun and adds a real dynamic to the early stages of a relationship.'

Do you think it's ever OK not to want to have sex with your girlfriend?

PETE B: 'It is OK not to want to have sex with your girlfriend. People have varyingly powerful sex drives. And there are the whims of arousal to take into account: sometimes you want sex; sometimes you don't, because you're tired, bloated after dinner, stressed, etc. I think some women assume that if their fella doesn't want to sleep with them, he has stopped fancying them. This isn't true. Desire wears off after a few months of a relationship, and arousal is often kick-started by wanting something you can't have, and if you have a girlfriend sex is too obtainable, so the urge is perhaps less powerful, but it doesn't mean the woman is suddenly unattractive and will always be so from then on. After a break of a week, or perhaps even less, lust can return as strong as it was at the very first.'

JAKE M: 'Yes. Sometimes you can be tired or need some space. This will happen in relationships at some point but, from my experience, it is rare. Again, this can be just one of those things.'

If you booty-call a girl, does it mean you aren't considering her as a potential girlfriend?

I find the following answers some of the most telling of the whole book, because the recurrence of the idea of 'girlfriend material' is so strong. Men have incredibly rigid ideas of what will make a good girl-friend, and they decide if we make the grade very early on. I know we will sleep with guys we don't really see as boyfriend material, but we at least consider the possibility that they might be, probably every time we enjoy a shag with them, and keep an open mind. Men's fixed ideas about who makes the grade or not as girlfriends is the reason we shouldn't waste our time waiting around for them to treat us the way we want. We can't woo them into it. This is also as good evidence as any that men can coldly separate an enjoyable sex act from respect or feeling for the person it was experienced with. I know some women can do the same; I find myself thinking again about the person, possibly with a trace of longing, if we've had good, friendly sex with a nice atmosphere.

ANTHONY A: 'When a guy is just feeling frisky, it should never in any way be taken that he might actually want to date that girl. There are plenty of girls I want to sleep with, but very few of them I would consider girlfriend material. Lest we forget, booty calls always occur at night, which in theory means you are drunk, bored or let down by another girl/date, and so suddenly become free for the night. Booty calls have nothing to do with your suitability to be a girlfriend. And think of it this way: if he really liked you, he would have arranged to see you already – not just arranged to get in your pants for a quick thrill.'

IAIN H: 'Er, yes. Obviously. It means you are considering them as a potential one-night stand. If you're considering someone as a potential girlfriend, you'll do it properly.'

WILL L: 'Basically, yes, you're not considering her as a girlfriend. This might not be the case if it is in the context of going out on proper dates with her over the same period. If a girl is looking for a boyfriend, it's a strategy which is likely to leave her disappointed. I've even used b-calls as a back-up – i.e. go out but fail to attract any action, so make a call at the end of the evening. Not very flattering for the girl involved!'

When you're single, do you prefer quantity over quality when it comes to sex?

IAIN H: 'Both, ideally. But it depends if you're single because you want to be single, or single while you're waiting to find the next relationship. If you've recently broken up with someone, having lots of ropy, low-quality sex can just make you feel worse.'

WILL L: 'It's got to be quantity! The two things go hand in hand anyway. The only way to guarantee you get some quality is having plenty of adventures. You don't get anywhere standing on the sidelines – and that's true whether you're happily single playing the field, or if you'd really like a girlfriend. In any case, being sexually inactive can give you prostate cancer and I wouldn't want to get that. There's no way I'd go for someone I didn't fancy though.'

How big an issue is performance anxiety when you're sleeping with someone for the first time?

ED G: 'It depends if you are after one night with her, or see it as a long-term thing. If it's one night, a lot of people will just be in it to enjoy it and be more relaxed. If you really like the girl then maybe it's different; you can get scared and not function perfectly.'

TOM L: 'Absolutely. Anyone who says it isn't is like someone claiming they're not afraid of death: either a fool or a liar. In fact, I think men don't just get performance anxiety the first time. They get it *every* time. Despite the stereotype that all men are just after their own selfish pleasure, it's been utterly driven into our heads that we must be obsessively dedicated to our partner. Flick through any men's mag at random and along with the obligatory article about putting on muscle you'll find about three on how to please your partner. The implication is that it's not manly *not* to focus on them.'

What does it mean when a guy can't come? He doesn't fancy the girl enough?

I hate it when this happens. It becomes a 'thing', and you can't talk about it, so of course you just keep going, trying to encourage him with little (fake) noises of enthusiasm. But by then it's too late, and if there wasn't much pressure before, there sure is now. Plus you get bored, and it hurts, and you just wonder why you're having such a chemistry failure. Is it that cellulite? Take heart – it's not. They fancy you if they're having sex with you, if only in the moment. It's a sensation issue (and a pressure issue).

ALEK M: 'No, it doesn't mean you don't fancy her enough. Dehydration, too much alcohol, too little sleep, etc: these all contribute to this. You wouldn't think this was a problem if you had just had sex and the second time the guy had difficulty coming, so why should it be an issue the first time? After all, women claim to enjoy sex without always coming. One of those things.'

DAN H: 'In my experience, if you are aroused enough to get a hard-on you're almost guaranteed to blow your load. But not if you're deprived of sensation (a thick condom, or being drunk). And I guess if some dudes have that problem it's the same as not being able to get an erection or premature ejaculation: pressure. The self-imposed pressure to perform, or most often really wanting to have great sex with someone you're really attracted to and might be falling in love with, and being struck with the emotional force and significance of such a moment. Basically, unless you're numbed somehow or on drugs, or buckling under the pressure to perform, you can't have sex with someone without fancying them.'

How adventurous do you expect/want a girl to be in bed?

JAMES H: 'I like a slut – who doesn't? I've done more or less every depraved thing you can think of (no, really). One relationship in particular was the source of much of this. I don't care that much for theatrics in bed – by which I mean screaming, writhing, etc. But being adventurous is essential. What's great about being sexually adventurous with someone is it's a bonding agent. The "yes, but it's our depravity" type of thing.'

PAUL O: 'I think you want a girl to be adventurous in bed; nothing worse than a girl who just sits there. That said, best to keep the demands for anal beads and dressing up like a cowgirl to get ridden hard under wraps for a few weeks first.'

THOUGHTS OF THE FUTURE/ CHOOSING A MATE

Men, bless them, are as serious about taking a relationship to the next step as they are about game-playing (and being players) in the early stages. I've commented throughout on the extraordinarily fixed ideas they have about who makes 'girlfriend material'. As you'll see from the responses below, the fixed ideas continue, affecting everything from when to introduce a girlfriend to friends and parents (and what it means), to what class a prospective partner must be, to who makes 'marriage material'.

When would you first introduce a girl to your parents or best friend, and what does it mean?

ANTHONY S: 'These days I would only take a girl to see Mum and Dad if I could see myself marrying her in the future. Now that I have got to 30, I find myself only looking at girls as possible wives, and if they aren't perfect enough for that, then they get moved to the other category, "sleep with but don't stay with". The parents never meet these ones. As for friends, I don't mind introducing girlfriends to them, as long as the girls are hot – it can't hurt to always be seen with a yummy little thing.'

OK. If he's putting off introducing you to his friends, it could be that he doesn't think you're hot enough for his standards. You could be his little secret. Remember that *Sex and the City* episode at the Chinese restaurant where guys took mistresses they were embarrassed about? Do you really want to be the not-hot-enough girlfriend? NO WAY. But . . .

'On the other hand, when I find a girl I really like it usually takes longer to introduce them to friends, probably because I don't want the girl I like to see what us lads are really like, so I keep them away. I also find I never go out with my friends and my girlfriend in a group, I prefer to keep it separate.'

ISHAN B: 'Because my best friend and I are so close I would probably introduce a girlfriend to him very early on. Thus it wouldn't be a very big deal, though getting his approval is absolutely vital. If he didn't like the girl, didn't think she was attractive, etc., it wouldn't likely bode well for her.

'My parents are a totally different story. Introducing someone to them is a very big step for me and definitely signals real seriousness about the person and the relationship. The timing can vary massively on that, but I'm a pretty intense person and tend to move very quickly when I know I'm into someone.'

GUY P: 'I've only ever introduced girlfriends to my parents once I'm secure we are a genuine couple. So I've never introduced someone I've just been dating and who I've no long-term wish to be with. With mates it's different and more relaxed, so, for example, I introduced my current girlfriend to my best friends after just three or four dates.'

What turns a girlfriend into marriage material for a man?

HENRY W: 'Strength of character, being a good person. Someone who could happily survive without you, but wants nevertheless – i.e. chooses – to be with you. The idea that you'd want your kids to have a mum like her, that she'll value and support you in your work, and that you could do the same for her and would be able to keep her happy when you're old and unattractive and probably quite annoying.'

MOSES B: 'If you get on with the family, that's a big thing. I've had girlfriends and never met the parents. I met my wife's parents early on, so it was like a letter of intent. The other thing is that you should get through the first six months without any arguments – it should be a clear run.'

Does it matter to you how rich or poor or what class a woman is?

LEE W: 'In theory, not at all. In reality, a lot. I have never
   gone out with someone from a completely different class
   background. It obviously plays no part in the kind of
   person you are, in all the important respects. But personally, all the small, seemingly insignificant, day-to-day
   aspects of life, e.g. drinking Earl Grey as a matter of course
   (I am middle class, can you tell?), really matter. However,
   the amount of money a person earns or possesses does not
   matter to me at all (as long as it's above zero). Have I
   redeemed myself?'

TOM E: 'Yes, I'm afraid it does. Class is not always important, but it has shaped our views of the world. Something
   I take for granted is that I will always have money. My
   parents have a lot of it. One day they will give it to me and
   my brother. Having a country house, a town house, fancy
   cars and all that – that's just something I grew up with.
   It's there. I can't imagine it not being there. I used to go
   out with someone who grew up in a much less advan-
   taged home. Suburban, blue collar, etc. I confess I felt very
   out of place when I was there. I think she felt the same
   way spending time at my parents' house, surrounded by
   my public school boy, stockbroker friends. I spent weekend after weekend at my then-girlfriend's house in the
   suburbs and, in short, I was uncomfortable. Monied people
   make me feel safe. I hate the way that sounds, but hating
   it doesn't make it untrue.'

Do you ever think consciously about whether your date would make a good mother to your children?

AMIR D: 'We always think that way. I wouldn't think about it on the first date, but I'm also a dreamer so I let myself think about the future all the time. I quite often sit there imagining a happy family with kids – it's the most important thing in life!'

LEE M: 'Of course! It's a completely natural and obvious thing to do: if you think they'd be a crap mother, then surely that tells you something fairly negative about your general opinion of them as a person. Also, there's clearly no serious "future" with that person if you can't, at least in principle, imagine yourself raising children with them . . . Unless you don't want kids, of course.'

JOHN S: 'Yes, but not in great detail.'

Do guys genuinely want to get married, or do they ask us just to keep us happy?

Most guys of our generation don't get all excited about marriage in the same way that many women do. Even when they're not opposed to it, they're not exactly into it. They just accept it as a necessary part of getting older. I think a lot of women are very familiar with faintly bewildered, heel-dragging behaviour from the groom-to-be, who often sees the wedding as a big painful mix of family and pointless spending. Funny when you consider it's usually men who propose.

It's also worth noting that I do know of a certain breed of traditional man who wants to get married because he has his eye on the perfect, keeping-up-appearances family lifestyle. And there is also the ugly guy who is so thrilled to have found someone he wants to make her his asap. These guys are all about popping the question.

But they're not the average modern twenty- to thirty-somethings
we meet on our rounds.

TIM S: 'Marriage: in brief, no, we don't believe in it and, yes,
we do ask to keep the woman happy. It's not that men are
cads; it's just that the institution inherently means less to
us than it does to women. I can understand why: it's that
old issue about women fearing their charms will decline as
they age, whereas men's will grow. They want some sort
of safety net, some support, some public pledge that their
fella's not going to run off with a young floozy. I think men
feel like, "Well, why don't you just trust me? Why do you
need this rather expensive symbol? Don't you believe I can
be true to you – and myself – without all this ceremony?"
Ultimately, though, we recognize that this is just the way
it is, and so men tend to marry because we know it will
comfort our partner rather than ourselves.'

DENNIS D: 'We believe in marriage, we're just not that
bothered about weddings. We don't have that whole
princess-for-a-day thing that you lot grow up with, so it's
all a bit of a burden. If maybe there was more party and
less organizing we would be, but there's not, so we aren't.

'But marriage is OK and I think we're happy to do it for
the same reason that we're happy to accept any other
curtailing of freedom: the terrifying fear of being old and
alone. There might not be as many men who're concerned
to be married with kids, but there's not that many fewer;
it's always curious to see how many guys do slip into
comfortable domesticity when the chance of it comes
along.

'The aging thing matters to us as well, of course. When

you're about 20, you're terrified of getting a girl pregnant; by your mid-20s you're still worried but not quite so haunted by it; and then sometime around 30 a certain type of man, perhaps one predisposed to fatalism, thinks, actually, maybe it wouldn't be such a bad thing at all. That's more to do with kids, obviously, but I think the marriage business works along similar lines: first you think somebody has to be perfect, then you realize no such person exists, and that's when you decide to be, and are, happy enough to marry.'

How important is it that your girlfriend has similar interests to you?

MATT D: 'To a limited degree. It's not so much fun if you like exactly the same stuff, because that's when things can get competitive too. It's the way you spend your time together that's most important, and I think that's broader than interests alone: are you both talkers, or do you like sitting around calmly, say; or how much do you both like to drink, and how do you like to do it. These things matter.'

TIM B: 'It helps, but it's not crucial. There are plenty of girls I know with whom I share far more interests than I do with my girlfriend, but I love her, and not them. Why? Who knows? There's just a connection sometimes that transcends interests. And from my past experience I've found it can actually become boring if you share too many interests in common. It's actually nice to be inexpert in something your partner knows plenty about. It's rather charming.'

ATTRACTION AND THE CHASE

Now, you could boil the whole dating game down to the chase. It's the elephant in the room until you're months in and farting in front of each other. Even then, there are still subtle negotiations for power. But in the early days, there are so many silent rules of etiquette designed to showcase each party in their best light: women as mysterious and not too keen; guys as chivalrous and charming. That's why the early days can be so painfully suspenseful – you haven't the least idea about what someone's thinking, so you're left trying to work it out based on signals and signs. Technically, when the chase is pursued properly, each side sticking to the rules to make the other work hard, a beautiful couple emerges. For men in particular, the chase is essential to the way they develop feelings (whereas if I fancy someone, I don't mind cutting *to* the chase). Time and time again they've told me that nothing's a bigger turn-off than a woman who defeats the chase by being too available. With guys who blow hot and cold, you reel 'em in by making them run after you. Just as long-distance runners love the challenge of a mara-thon, men love the women they can't have – without a fight, at least. Whether you're a hardcore game player or someone who just tries to keep the interest up through the first few dates as best you can, read on for the male view on some of those things you've wondered about in the chase stage. The mechanics of early dating, if you will.

As for attraction – what is it that turns men on or off? It can feel like the lottery. I for one have often stood by sniffing moodily while a plain-looking girl has swarms of men round her. Who can explain the attraction? Is it confidence or quietness? Sexiness? Is it curves or boyish skinniness that does it for them? Read on.

Could you ever fancy a large/fat woman?

Men don't care so much that you're skinny for its own sake – they look for packages – but they do seem to care about healthiness from an evolutionary perspective and otherwise. These days, bad diet can be a turn-off. But see the related question about curves and plumpness: several guys, such as Dennis here, say that there's a pressure to like the *FHM* type, but in reality a lot of guys like a bit of flesh and are just too embarrassed to admit it. Here are two perspectives, one from a clever, mature and lovely thirty-something with a realistic, respectful attitude towards women (Dennis), and another, equally prevalent view from a shallow woman-chaser who rarely manages to maintain a long-term relationship.

DENNIS D: 'Loads of guys do, and I think they fall into two camps: the ones where it's pretty much fetishistic, and the ones where guys just kind of prefer it, or are not too bothered either way. I think way more men like big girls than are comfortable admitting it, for fear of mockery. It falls into the category of instantly piss-takeable things, like ginger hair or sporting ineptitude. For sure, many men do want the *FHM/Nuts*-sanctioned idea of women (both in terms of their appearance and their seeming availability), but look at lots of happy couples and see how often men are with girls bigger than the media-decreed norm. For most sane men, being comfortable and enjoying your time together is the dominant factor in the success of a relationship. We don't want to go out for a meal with somebody who fusses and picks the healthiest, most joyless thing on the menu; we want to go out with somebody who clears their plate, has a pudding and a few glasses of wine and enjoys it all. Although we basically understand the self-denying nature of female existence, it still mystifies and terrifies us, so even if we do, in principle, like the end result, we don't like it enough to have to see the process. It's like watching sausages being made.'

This is so typical of the way a whole bunch of men think; they are fundamentally quite tolerant. They don't get put off by the imperfections we spend so much time and money battling. Remember that, ladies. A nice guy wants a nice girl who doesn't take herself too seriously. You heard Dennis! They would like us to be perfect, but not so much that they want to watch us flagellating ourselves to get there. Pie-on. Well, that's unless you fancy a guy like Alex . . .

ALEX A: 'I have no interest in fat women. For me it shows they are unhealthy, not suitable to be a prospective mother to my child, inactive, lazy and have a poor diet – all things which I find a turn-off. Plus, boys are brought up these days on a diet of glamour girls and Victoria's Secret shapes, which is very rare of course, but if you look hard enough you can find a little gem here or there. I have been lucky enough to go out with some girls with fabulous bodies, which is why I am such a shallow picky boy. That said, I can't help what I find attractive; she just happens to usually have great legs, peachy ass, nice boobs and a pretty face.'

Fair enough. So if you're plumpish then you might not get together with an Alex, whose 'diet' is Victoria's Secret rather than reality. Probably that's not the end of the world.

How do you feel about a girl taking the initiative, i.e. getting your number, asking you out, etc.?

Now, this is a funny one. It totally contradicts all the guff about the chase. Yet every guy said the same thing, i.e., yes, we love a girl who makes the move. I kept asking because it didn't seem to fit with everything else. And the guys kept saying the same thing, no matter who I asked. I've included three answers below to prove it. So it looks like both things are true: you have to let them chase you, but they also love it if you go for them. Tim B makes a good point, though: being forward only works if they fancy you. I say, once you've reeled them in through your own efforts, that's when you need to take the step back. There is no getting away from the need to hold something back. I stand by that.

TIM B: 'How do I feel about it? I think it's brilliant! Don't know why women are so ashamed about doing this. It's just about every guy's fantasy, in fact. It's only too forward if you're not actually all that keen on the woman. If you like her, then can it work from there? Absolutely.'

JON S: 'Absolutely fine. In fact, much to be encouraged.'

JAMES B: 'God, who doesn't love a girl taking initiative? It's wonderful. You don't have to be Samantha Jones, but having a sense of what you want is very sexy and, more importantly, attractive. As I've got older, I've got better at sleeping with women – and one of the things I've learnt is that not trying to sleep with someone is a really good way of getting them to sleep with you. If you're gorgeous you can do whatever you want, but most of us aren't. So letting a girl have control is a great technique.'

Note to anyone who claims men don't think: is this not evidence to the contrary? A red-blooded guy like James *consciously* plays a sophisticated power game to make us more inclined to sleep with him.

Do you always pay for everything on the first few dates and why?

I find it a massive turn-off if the guy lets me pay on the first date. Actually, make that the first few. And yet when they do pay I'm always touched, and wonder how they know to do it, and what they think when they do.

AMIR D: 'I'm always paying. Not because I'm a show-off; it's just my nature, and I have the option.'

ALEX R: 'I would always offer to pay for a first date; however, I've had a fair few experiences where this has either set an uncomfortable precedent or has caused unexpected friction. In the right context it's a lovely old-fashioned gesture which can be rather romantic, but if sharing the expense is more appropriate then I'd always consider conceding.'

KEITH B: 'One of the best things a girl can do is pay all or some of her way – or offer to pay, or occasionally buy the groceries, the wine, the cab ride. I couldn't be further from cheap, but it's so nice when a girl says, "No, I want to get this . . ."'

Is it true that men prefer blondes?

MATT F: 'No, I'm not fussed. You look for the whole package. I think girls are most attractive when they have a coherent look or style. I'm totally not into dyed platinum blonde or blatantly dyed hair of any colour. Generally speaking I think blondes had their time during Pamela Anderson's heyday in the mid 90s, but a bombshell's a bombshell!'

PETER J: 'Not in my case. For some reason, it's redheads who turn my head. I wasn't aware of this until a few years ago, when I noticed I would gaze at auburn locks on the Tube, and begin to fantasize about romance. Yes, and it was romance as well as lust, whereas blonde, for some reason, only seems to trigger the latter. All four of my serious long-term relationships have been with women with green eyes or red hair, and two of them had both.'

How important is the chase?

DANNY J: 'Very. In the words of some American football coach, it's not everything, it's the only thing. So when I was younger and more idealistic and even more confused by everything than I am now, I thought about how much better life would be without the game-playing, feints, dummies, obfuscation and deceit of courtship, and imagined a bright future society of honesty and clarity. I was quite a naive and hopeless lad. After years of waiting for this to happen, and it not, I realized that, first of all, you have to play the game. It's not that there's some pure love out there where you can sidestep all that and get straight to unalloyed joy and intimacy. I also realized that game-playing's a test to weed out the nutters.'

MARK F: 'Dangerously so. I always found that the chase was important in the sense that it could have a big impact on how you felt. But I always worried that the excitement of the chase tended to impair my ability to judge whether I was genuinely into the person I was chasing. I think people should treat their attitudes during the chase with suspicion.'

Does it put you off if a girl seems to be following some rule, such as 'only kiss/shag after the third date'?

VICTOR L: 'I would throw up. Maybe hold back on the first, but on the second you gotta kiss. I hate people who play games. What's the point? The only type of game is to just keep restraining yourself. That's it! It's the same in business: if I have a client I want to do business with, I keep it really chilled.'

ALLEN P: 'It certainly can put you off. I once dated a girl who only "made up her mind" after a minimum of fifteen dates. We lasted three before I made up my mind independently. If it's an indicator of a reserved personality then that's entirely fair enough, and a degree of reserve and enigma is actually quite attractive to me. However, if it's for the sake of following an arbitrary rule read in a magazine or self-imposed without consideration to an obvious feeling or atmosphere, then that can be a massive turn-off.'

Do you find quiet women mysterious or intimidating?

JOHN S: 'Depends on how the quietness manifests itself. Coy smiles and modesty, etc., can be very alluring, but intense staring, etc., expecting you (the man) to do all the work, is very off-putting.'

DENNIS D: 'I think first of all we need to add another category: boring. Speaking as quite a rustic, straightforward man, I find the quiet thing – especially if it's an affected attempt to foster a sense of mystery – tiresome and frustrating. Flirting requires a lot of words and a lot of chance-taking, so quiet women (or men) can't be doing that – and it's one of the great joys of life. Intimidating is, I suppose, a different matter. Again speaking very personally, I only get really intimidated by incredibly efficient, businesswomen kind of women, or very vulgar girls who scare me with their depraved wit. Also, when a woman is talkative it tells you that she is not so concerned about appearances (her own, but also yours) as to see keeping quiet as the best strategy. Which is nice.'

Do you like a woman to be talkative on a date?

AMIR D: 'Very much so. I need her to be talkative and open or else I get bored. Simple as that.'

ALEX A: 'It's very important that a girl is talkative on the date, otherwise you have to just sit there and feel like it's an interview. Then you find as a boy you end up just talking about yourself all night. You need a balance.'

What have you felt when you've found out a friend fancies you?

Oh, the nightmare of falling in love with a friend who does not feel the same way. See the Charlie Files in Chapter 15 for an in-depth look at why guys, on the whole, aren't in favour of turning friendships into something more.

GARY P: 'It depends on the desirability of the fancier. Mostly I guess it's flattering; rarely is it a surprise. "Friends who fall in love" is a great story – maybe it drives friendships at some level. I've slept with a lot of my friends over the years. And girls being girls tend to like sleeping with guys they know. It also has the added advantage of enabling me to sleep with women who are much better looking than me.'

DON L: 'Actually, this happened to me for the first time recently. And to make it more complicated she is a colleague as well as a friend. And the truth is I don't feel the same way and I feel shit about it. And she was totally sober when she told me. It did concern me when she said she had started to close down relationships when they didn't match up to me. I personally wouldn't have the guts to say it if I had those feelings for a friend and wasn't sure they were reciprocated.'

And finally, this question doesn't fit anywhere in particular, but I think it's a goodie, so here it is:

How do you feel about going shopping with your girlfriend?

DARREN P: 'I feel like screaming and throwing a tantrum of boredom every time I go shopping with a woman, any woman. It's horrific. Men buy stuff they want, and they know before they go anywhere what they are going to buy, how much it costs and where it is. That means that if you have to go up town to get it, you are up there and back with military precision. Not a moment is wasted, not a step. No distractions. Want it, find it, get it, go home. Women are not like this and it's awful to sit through.'

Conclusion

So what have we gained from all this? I hope that it's the reassuring revelation that men are, in fact, not aliens, and that finding an amazing one need not be out of reach. In fact, there are amazing guys locked up in some of those dudes who act all weirdly to us. In certain circumstances, armed with an insight into how his mind works, we can even unlock and unleash Mr Amazing and live happily ever after. But that's getting ahead of ourselves a bit.

By candidly sharing their views on dating and love, the hundreds of guys I've talked to have shown that many of the stereotypes that define them – such as being careless, thoughtless sex-machines – just aren't true. For example, it lightened my heart to find out that the purchase of a toothbrush can symbolize years of carefully planned validation-hunting (Christian) or that a guy who's reluctant to move in with his girlfriend may be waiting for a sign from the gods that she's the one (Ben).

That is, there is always, always a reason for blokes' behaviour; he is always (well, usually) actively thinking something. More times than not, it's something to do with his ego, whether that's an arrogant fear that he'll break your heart beyond repair by splitting up with you, or buttering you up to suit his short-term sex drive.

Then there's the fact that their thinking patterns aren't entirely dissimilar to ours. Like Aaron, haven't you ever enjoyed bantering but figured it was time to get going once it looked as though things might get physical? Or strung someone along to keep your options open out of a fear of being alone, like Nadav in the quick-fire question on page 143?

Even more curiously, it seems that lots of guys are actually more sensitive than us. They find it harder to move on after a break-up, and feel more agony, owing to the grips of their big egos, and of course to performance anxiety, than we do. Think of poor Dan and his failure to get over Sally five years down the line. Or Joe, who despite ending it with Jessica, developed an all-consuming possessiveness over her because he couldn't cope with having lost control. The urge to be needed and approved of is incredibly strong – so strong that guys are willing to spend thousands on a girl just to make her want to marry him before he ditches her for the next one.

They're not all sweet and troubled, though. That bewildering cold-ness men sometimes show us – and that we try to excuse as 'fear' or 'confusion' – is really there, rock-hard and terrifying. It's in every single guy, although at different times. Even the nicest men on the feedback panel had shudderingly icy things to say about certain situations. Tom L, for instance, revealed that he could see why a feeling of hatred was ignited in Justin when he was woken by Lexie looking for a cuddle. Adam Lyons, the professional pick-up artist, shed the starkest light on myste-rious masculine behaviour: some (like Christian) are motivated purely by the desire to be needed and manage to form not an ounce of attach-ment in going about achieving their goal. Barry, on the panel, explained Steve's freak-outs at the one-year mark as boredom and disgust with his girlfriend and a yearning for the multiple fucks of singledom. This may not have been the reason for Steve's behaviour, but it shows just how scarily even a sweet and smiley man like Barry can think.

Knowing all this should help you to get more out of your relationships with men, regardless of how serious they are about you. It'll help you to better spend your time and energy (wit, charm, affection) by knowing who is worth your time and why, and who is a dead end and emotionally negative for you. You'll therefore be freer for all the truly enjoyable, life-affirming flings, fucks, affairs and relationships that are within your grasp.

And how do you tell when a guy is just a no-hoper, and when you're more likely to get what you want from a brick wall than from him? Well, this book should help you to tell which key force is governing his odd behaviour, whether it's the need for constant validation (Christian), a fear of growing up (Ben), a fear of losing his freedom (Martin), an obsession with novelty (Frank), a lack of sexual interest in you (Raphael), his ego (Seb) or a fear of losing control (Joe). Once you've identified which it is, you can decide what to do. Of the above, for example, Christian, Frank and Raphael are the ones I'd tell you to run screaming from without a glance back. Unless you're a sucker for self-harm. But the great thing about figuring a man out is that it gives you control over who you decide to put effort into and who you send packing with a great, bellowing, 'Next!' When you know what a man is thinking, you're in charge.

But it's not all about getting rid of no-hopers. It's about knowing when and how to persevere with guys who you really like and who may well turn out to be winners too. The whole 'he's just not that into you' thing is patently oversimplistic. That creed suggests you should give up on countless situations that aren't immediately perfect through and through. But in some situations, you can find a way around a guy's mental block or issue and it's really worth it. Take the example of Ben and Julia (Chapter 6): Ben wouldn't move in with Julia, but after smart action on Julia's part, Ben came crawling back saying that he missed her. Julia refused to get back together with him until they'd really had it out, with Ben coming clean about his anxieties and fears about moving in, and the result was that he was clear in his mind about wanting Julia. Julia eventually realized that his fears were huge, ingrained and not to do with her – forcing him to recognize this won the day. I am pleased to be able to report that they eventually moved in together and are still happily domesticating it up.

Then there's Mark and Vicky. Remember how he saw her as less than a girlfriend but more than a fuck-buddy? And how her adoration for him stopped her telling him that this wasn't good enough? Well, after she ended it (he made her do so by being so rubbish), it wasn't long before he started to miss the sex. They started meeting up, but Vicky refused to be whatever Mark wanted her to be – something that suited his needs – when she had real feelings for him. She told him she felt a lot for him and that either he was going to offer her a relationship or they were not going to be in touch. He chose the relationship.

There's a lot of fun and love to be had. What we women aren't always great at is knowing when to lay down the line and give an ultimatum. But if there are two pieces of advice to take from all this, it's these. First, allow a reasonable chase time by holding back: the vast majority of men say that on one hand they're not crazy about games, but on the other it's off-putting if a woman is too available. In chasing a bit, and winning the chase, men feel an exalted sense of achievement – the degree to which depends on the kind of guy you're after. But even the well-spoken gentlemen who seem anything other than egomaniacal womanizers admit to preferring someone who keeps something back in the early days. Second, if it's not going the way you want after a few months, tell him that, offer to leave and mean it. It's one thing to feel messed around by guys; it's another to sell yourself short. And there's no need. After all, you're dating to feel happy and to enhance your life, right? So go forth and enjoy.

Acknowledgements

Thanks to Jenny Lord at Fig Tree for encouraging me to write this book, for being such a superb editor and ideas-woman, and for inspiring me with lots of fascinating romantic dilemmas. To Hannah Westley, who recruited me for the column in *thelondonpaper* after hearing me complain venomously about the inscrutable behaviour of a guy I was obsessed with. To Maor for encouraging me to spend a year writing about my experiences with other men, and for providing some valuable insights into the male mind. To my girlfriends, who supported me, told me their tales, inspired me with their woes and successes, and made sure I wrote about real issues that they – and you – care about. Jo, Natalie (hello, Maureen), Lexie, Daniela: you were all great. Tom Stammers, thank you for having a brainwave or two along the way; they made all the difference. And last but very, very far from least, thanks to the men who made this book possible, by explaining their actions so beautifully, honestly and illuminatingly. There was no incentive for them to spill the beans, apart from the desire to increase the understanding between the sexes, and they helped do it big time.

Adam Lyons lent his professional eye generously and sharply, and was formative in my understanding of male players and how to spot them. His website is: www.attractionexplained.com. Anthony, Tom, Andrew, Victor, Dennis, Jon and Nadav, thank you all in particular.

Calling all girls!

It's the invitation of the season.

Penguin books would like to invite you to become a member of Bijoux – the exclusive club for anyone who loves to curl up with the hottest reads in fiction for women.

You'll get all the inside gossip on your favourite authors – what they're doing, where and when; we'll send you early copies of the latest reads months before they're on the High Street and you'll get the chance to attend fabulous launch parties!

And, of course, we realise that even while she's reading every girl wants to look her best, so we have heaps of beauty goodies to pamper you with too.

If you'd like to become a part of the exclusive world of Bijoux, email
bijoux@penguin.co.uk

Bijoux books for Bijoux girls

He just wanted a decent book to read ...

Not too much to ask, is it? It was in 1935 when Allen Lane, Managing Director of Bodley Head Publishers, stood on a platform at Exeter railway station looking for something good to read on his journey back to London. His choice was limited to popular magazines and poor-quality paperbacks – the same choice faced every day by the vast majority of readers, few of whom could afford hardbacks. Lane's disappointment and subsequent anger at the range of books generally available led him to found a company – and change the world.

'We believed in the existence in this country of a vast reading public for intelligent books at a low price, and staked everything on it'
Sir Allen Lane, 1902–1970, founder of Penguin Books

The quality paperback had arrived – and not just in bookshops. Lane was adamant that his Penguins should appear in chain stores and tobacconists, and should cost no more than a packet of cigarettes.

Reading habits (and cigarette prices) have changed since 1935, but Penguin still believes in publishing the best books for everybody to enjoy. We still believe that good design costs no more than bad design, and we still believe that quality books published passionately and responsibly make the world a better place.

So wherever you see the little bird – whether it's on a piece of prize-winning literary fiction or a celebrity autobiography, political tour de force or historical masterpiece, a serial-killer thriller, reference book, world classic or a piece of pure escapism – you can bet that it represents the very best that the genre has to offer.

Whatever you like to read – trust Penguin.